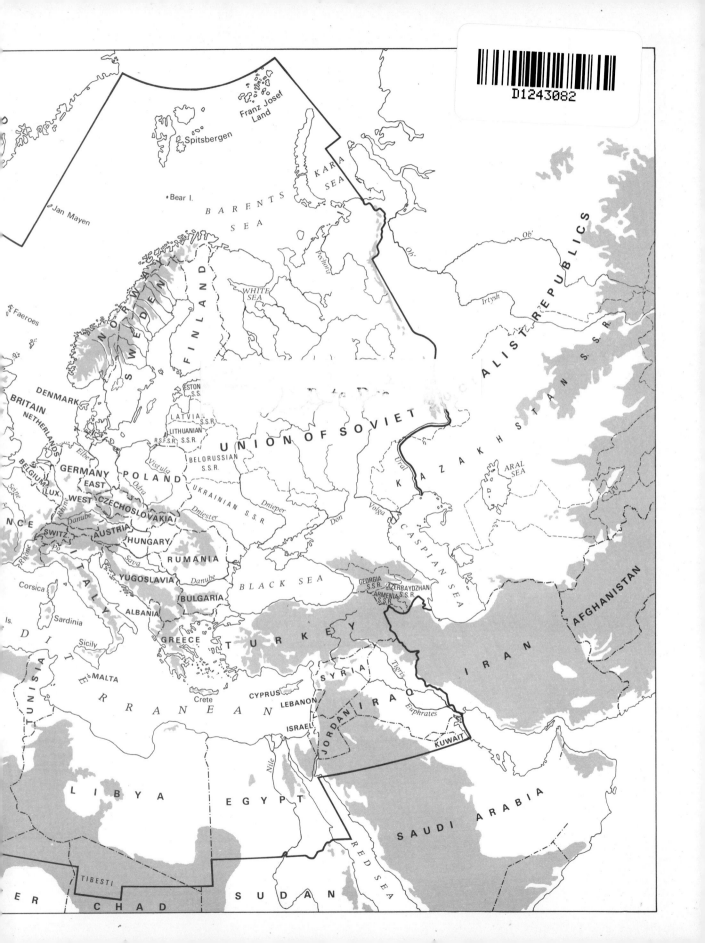

Franz Josef
Land

Spitsbergen

• Bear I.

• Jan Mayen

KARA
SEA

BARENTS
SEA

Ob'

Pechora

Irtysh

° Faeroes

WHITE
SEA

ALIST REPUBLICS

DENMARK

BRITAIN

NETHERLANDS

NORWAY

SWEDEN

FINLAND

ESTON.
S.S.R.

LATVIA
S.S.R.

LITHUANIAN
S.S.R.

R.S.F.S.R.

BELORUSSIAN
S.S.R.

UNION OF SOVIET

KAZAKHSTAN S.S.R.

Ob'

ARAL
SEA

BELGIUM

LUX.

GERMANY

EAST

WEST

POLAND

Elbe

Odra

Vistula

UKRAINIAN S.S.R.

Dnieper

Dniester

Don

Volga

Ural

NCE

CZECHOSLOVAKIA

Danube

Rhine

SWITZ.

AUSTRIA

HUNGARY

Po

Sava

RUMANIA

Danube

CASPIAN SEA

ITALY

Rhone

YUGOSLAVIA

BLACK SEA

GEORGIA
S.S.R.

AZERBAYDZHAN
S.S.R.

ARMENIA
S.S.R.

AFGHANISTAN

Corsica

BULGARIA

Is.

Sardinia

ALBANIA

GREECE

TURKEY

IRAN

Sicily

MALTA

Crete

CYPRUS

SYRIA

Tigris

LEBANON

DIT

R R A N E A N

ISRAEL

JORDAN

IRAQ

Euphrates

KUWAIT

TUNISIA

Nile

SAUDI   ARABIA

LIBYA

EGYPT

RED SEA

TIBESTI

ER

CHAD

SUDAN

Birds of Prey of
Britain and Europe

Birds of Prey of Britain and Europe

Ian Wallace

Paintings by
Ian Willis

Oxford New York

OXFORD UNIVERSITY PRESS

1983

Oxford University Press, Walton Street, Oxford OX2 6DP

London Glasgow New York Toronto
Delhi Bombay Calcutta Madras Karachi
Kuala Lumpur Singapore Hong Kong Tokyo
Nairobi Dar es Salaam Cape Town
Melbourne Auckland
and associates in
Beirut Berlin Ibadan Mexico City Nicosia

Oxford is a trade mark of Oxford University Press

Published in the United States
by Oxford University Press, New York

British Library Cataloguing in Publication Data
Wallace, Ian
Birds of Prey of Britain and Europe.
1. Birds of prey—Europe
I. Title
598'.91'094   QL696.F3
ISBN 0–19–217729–X

Set by Oxford Publishing Services, Oxford
Printed in Hong Kong

Foreword

by Stanley Cramp

The diurnal birds of prey form a closely related group of some 290 species, often considered to belong to one order, the Falconiformes, although some taxonomists favour splitting them into several orders. They are widespread almost throughout the world, with 50 species occurring in Europe, North Africa, and the Middle East, but only 37 in Europe. They are often superb birds, appealing to many because of their powerful flight and their evocation of wild places, although some species have long been persecuted by a powerful minority. Ornithologists have studied them intensively, especially in recent years, and much is known of their habits, behaviour, and numbers. Yet for the birdwatcher in the field, the identification of some species, especially those on migration, still presents a considerable challenge. The aim of this work is to illustrate, in colour, the 50 species to be seen in Europe and adjacent areas, and to summarize the main aspects of their identification and biology. The plates, by Ian Willis, are taken from the second volume of the *Handbook of the Birds of Europe, the Middle East and North Africa : The Birds of the Western Palearctic* (1980), a seven volume work now being published by the Oxford University Press. The text is by D.I.M. Wallace, a keen amateur bird-watcher and the author of several books and many papers on field identification. He is also one of the Editors of *The Birds of the Western Palearctic*, Volume II, on which his text is largely based, and which readers who desire fuller information on any aspect should consult.

There is little doubt that many of the diurnal birds of prey in Europe and adjacent areas have suffered a catastrophic decline in numbers in historic times. This decline is due almost entirely to the influence of man, whether direct or indirect. Man's attitude to predators has always been ambivalent. He has admired them for their strength and magnificent way of flight, depicting eagles, e.g. on royal standards and medieval coats of arms, yet he has ruthlessly persecuted them because they were thought to threaten his poultry or because they offered large and impressive targets for his guns.

Formerly such persecution had little effect on numbers because weapons were too little developed for any mass slaughter. This changed gradually and the development of breech-loading guns in the nineteenth century led to a rapid decline in many raptors over the whole of Europe, linked as it was with the growth of game preservation and well-keepered estates. One expert (see Bijleveld 1974) estimated that in 1965 the numbers of European birds of prey amounted to only 1 per cent of their population in the early nineteenth century. Three examples from Britain illustrate this. The Red Kite, once widespread and a common scavenger even in Elizabethan London, was reduced to a tiny remnant in central Wales and only rigorous protection has enabled this remnant to survive and, in recent years, increase slightly. The White-tailed Eagle, once not uncommon in Scotland (and Ireland), with a few pairs in England, became extinct after about 1916 because of ruthless persecution and, in the later stages, the activities of egg-collectors. The Buzzard, also once widespread in Britain, became extinct over much of its range in the nineteenth century but since 1914 has recovered somewhat (despite a temporary decline due to myxomatosis in rabbits, an important prey). It is still absent over large areas of eastern and central England where illegal persecution continues (see Moore 1957). Many similar examples could be quoted for the rest of Europe, and the tragic and horrifying details of the ruthless slaughter of most predators in the last 150 years have been given by Bijleveld (1974). Despite the volume of scientific studies which have shown that predatory birds rarely have any serious impact on game populations, many owners of property or their gamekeepers still regard them as harmful and kill them by various means, although many of these birds are now protected by law in most European countries.

The other direct human impacts are much slighter but can have a critical effect when the numbers of a species have fallen to a low level. The first is egg-collecting, which in Britain played a key part in the extinction of both Osprey and White-tailed Eagle; unfortunately, there has been a revival of this dangerous and usually illegal hobby in recent years, especially in Britain. The second is the ancient sport of falconry which had a marginal effect when birds of prey were numerous, but with their decline has become a serious threat to some species, such as the Peregrine. It should be said that responsible falconers readily accept the need for restrictions on use and other conservation measures. There are, unfortunately, still some who break the law, e.g. robbing nests or taking part in the lucrative trade in the larger falcons.

The indirect effects of man's activities are mostly of lesser importance. Most serious was the use of persistent pesticides after 1945, which caused the deaths of adult birds of many species and also reduced fertility due to thin eggshells and behavioural disturbances. The results were catastrophic for some species in both Europe and North America—notably the Peregrine (which became extinct within eastern North America and showed a 50 per cent drop in Britain, with barely a quarter of the survivors managing to rear any young), the Golden Eagle, the White-tailed Eagle, the Sparrowhawk, and, especially in the USA, the Osprey. In recent years severe restrictions on the use of these organochlorines have led to some recovery of all these species in many areas. Habitat changes have not been as serious for predators as for some other birds (e.g. those breeding in wetlands), but the larger birds of prey often nest in wild country and many suffer from increased disturbance from tourists, including bird-watchers. Finally, one group has been harmed by changes in pastoral methods; the vultures, which in southern Europe are important scavengers of domestic animals, have seen this food supply diminished markedly with more hygienic modern practices.

Much is being done for Europe's birds of prey. Man's attitude to them has changed greatly in recent years, and many countries, but by no means all, offer full protection to all species, while international trade in the rarer ones is more strictly controlled. However, law-breaking still occurs, even in Britain, where some species continue to be shot, trapped, and poisoned, or robbed of eggs and young. Several countries employ wardens to safeguard the nests of rarer species, while in others artificial food supplies are provided for the threatened vultures. The outlook, however, for many larger predators is still gloomy and renewed efforts are essential if these magnificent creatures are to continue to grace the skies of Europe.

Contents

An introduction to the birds of prey

INTRODUCTION AND CLASSIFICATION

The diurnal birds of prey are quick, sudden beings—often nowhere but high in the sky or nothing but a dot on a far horizon—and their certain identification and close observation are two of the hardest and most complex tasks in field ornithology. Not surprisingly they have increasingly attracted a specialized literature, currently culminating most effectively not in the ordinary field guides but, for all the European and West Palearctic species, in the second volume of *The Birds of the Western Palearctic*.

This book has firm roots in the classic work just mentioned, but it is written for any observer or admirer of these superb birds who may be confronted by a strange hawk or falcon and wishes to know its name and something of its way of life. It concentrates, therefore, on providing written vignettes of each species opposite the plates of perched birds and fuller notes on flight behaviour and appearance opposite the plates of flying ones. Before these are reached, however, the general raptorial scene is set by essays which illuminate the birds' classification and evolution, their habitat preferences, their populations and movements, their food, their social patterns and behaviour, their breeding biology, their plumages and moults, and finally their interactions with man. In the main, subjects requiring lengthy transcriptions or measurements are omitted, but some references to them are given in the form of examples.

Hopefully the texts will suffice to sharpen interest in, and spur fuller attention to, some of the most fascinating and majestic birds upon this earth—many of which are under serious threat. For the illustrations the claim for their content can be set higher. All come from the eye and hand of Ian Willis, the observer artist responsible for all the plates in *The Birds of the Western Palearctic* and in the best of the recent identification guides, *Flight Identification of European Raptors* (Porter, Willis, Christensen, and Nielsen 1981). Their pedigree is therefore excellent.

To many, the term 'bird of prey' and its alternative, 'raptor', include the Strigiformes or mainly nocturnal owls. They are, however, excluded here; the diurnal birds of prey form the subjects of this book. In the most general sense they are avian species that find, hunt, and kill other animals for food; in the least general sense, they belong, in the Old World, to two closely related avian orders, the Accipitriformes and the Falconiformes. With hawking or falconry, a human pursuit for over 3000 years, the basic division of the two orders had been long recognized, but it took the improved scientific classification of the eighteenth century and onwards to confirm and define their true dichotomy beyond the ancient groups of rather 'utilitarian' short-winged hawks and more 'noble' long-winged falcons. The raptorial branches of the avian tree still tend to wave in the systematic winds of change, but there is now general acceptance that throughout the world there are five distinct families of diurnal birds of prey. These are the Cathartidae or New World vultures, of which there are seven species, the Sagittaridae with one species, the Secretary Bird of Africa, the Accipitridae or hawks, Old World vultures and harriers, in which conglomerate there are about 220 species, the Pandionidae with one species, the cosmopolitan fish-eating Osprey, and the Falconidae or falcons and caracaras, of which there are 61 species. Thus the total world diversity of diurnal raptors comes to about 290 species.

Of the above total, the West Palearctic harbours only 50 members of the Accipitridae, Pandionidae, and Falconidae. Thus in English terms, Europeans, North Africans, and the peoples of the Middle East need look out only for five main groups of raptors: the kites and hawks, the vultures, the eagles, the Osprey, and the falcons. More strictly, Europeans are concerned with 37 species, of which only 14 are widespread.

As with many populous non-passerine orders, size, form, and appearance vary widely in diurnal raptors. Contrast, for example, the huge Lammergeier weighing up to 7.5 kg with the tiny Shikra weighing no more than 275 g. Yet a closer look shows that they, and all their West Palearctic relatives, share common features determined by their carnivorous diet. Of these, the most striking is the savage, raptorial bill which is always hooked downwards on the upper mandible. Traditionally mentioned next are the powerful feet and talons required for the killing and gripping of prey and to allow the tearing beak a good purchase. These are, however, not universally well-developed and in the scavenging species such as vultures they may well have never developed (or regressed) as their specialization proceeded and other features such as bare heads and necks became more efficient adaptations to carrion eating. Then there are the more obvious external structural similarities such as the relatively long and often broad wings and tails required for various, frequently combined modes of flight that allow first the finding and then the successful capture of prey. Thus nearly all diurnal birds of prey have the ability to soar and glide effortlessly, even to hang on the wind, and also to stoop at or chase down fast-flying or -running prey. This is no mean skill but, once again, the carrion feeders lack the latter features as their need is constantly to travel far in search of corpses.

Less obvious, but as crucial to their mode of life as the above features, are the eyes of diurnal raptors. They are proportionately huge and afford excellent vision, with their exceptional acuity directly related to the presence of additional foveae and the greatest density of retinal cones in all vertebrates. Their hearing is also good, particularly in the owl-faced harriers *Circus*, and thus their overall powers of perception are extremely acute.

The adaptations discussed above, and others, make most diurnal birds of prey efficient predators, but their easy survival is hampered by more than man's hand. Some are temperamental breeders, sensitive to fluctuations in prey species and carrion sources, and most are slow breeders, not becoming sexually active for several years, having specialized nest requirements and rearing only one brood of slow-growing, often competitive young. No wonder that even the most ardent and skilled conservationist crosses his fingers. Because of breeding factors, most noticeably those related to tainted food, raptor fortunes can be brought to a sudden threshold of total danger in a relatively short period of persecution or toxicological accident. Peace, open horizons, and large areas of wilderness make up most of their natural places; and there are, therefore, clear ecological themes in their distribution, from which only a few species have achieved successful adaptations in the face of changing agricultural practices and urban development.

As already noted, the systematic classification of diurnal raptors is still disputed but certain assemblages are readily grouped by a combination of form, appearance, and behaviour. The following notes attempt to define the characters of the orders, families and genera occurring in the West Palearctic—Europe, North Africa, and the Middle East.

Order ACCIPITRIFORMES

Containing all West Palearctic raptors except the falcons.

Family Accipitridae

Containing all hawks, eagles, and Old World vultures.

Genus *Pernis* This genus comprises the so-called 'honey buzzards', of which two or three only mildly predatory species are recognized. They are confined to Old World forests, and within such habitat they exist mainly on a diet of social insects. In the search for this unusual diet, the honey buzzards have become expert watchers and followers of flying insects, landing in trees or on the ground to dig out nests and eat or carry off the larvae to their nestlings. They can also take insects in flight, in a more traditionally hawk-like manner, but their occasional fondness for fruit only serves to stress their departure from a typically raptorial diet which shows only in the theft of small mammal and bird young. Although their general form and appearance closely resembles that of the true buzzards (see *Buteo*), their flight action recalls that of the kites (see *Milvus*) and certain adaptations assist their dietary specialization directly. The birds are protected from stings by dense, scale-like feathers on their foreheads, have powerful feet and only slightly curved talons for digging, and breathe through narrow slits clearly adapted to prevent soil blockage. Honey buzzards exploit similar nest sites to buzzards but have a habit of persistently decorating them with tree foliage, usually of their favourite beech. They lay a clutch of usually two eggs and time the fledging of their young to the maximum availability of insect larvae. All are highly migratory, wintering over and in African and south Asian forests. In Europe, this small, very specialized genus of near-kite raptors is represented by the Honey Buzzard.

Genus *Elanus* This genus includes the smaller kites, of which up to five species are recognized. They stem from savanna habitats mainly in the southern hemisphere and there they hunt ground prey. To find such, they have developed hunting methods that combine the hovering of kestrels (see *Falco*) with the quartering of harriers (see *Circus*), and forms that include a broad, rather owl-like head and pale plumage patterns that are cryptic against the sky. Although many raptors show bright orange-yellow irises, these birds have carmine-red ones. For nest-sites, they choose densely foliaged trees and bushes; they build their own nests, lay three or four eggs, and raise young whose first plumages show above a relict scaled pattern that hints at a once close relationship to other small raptors. All are at least partly migratory or dispersive, seeking out the denser populations of their prey over wide areas. In Europe, this genus is represented by the beautiful Black-winged kite.

Genus *Milvus* This genus contains only two species but they are widely recognized as large, 'classic' kites in both the avian and human history of the Old World. Both are adaptable raptors and have long left their ancestral forest niches to exploit the food provided by natural carrion or human waste, though as yet without any marked easing of their breeding requirements. Their search for young animals in short, often aquatic, cover is aided by one of the supreme aerial forms, with long, flexible wings complemented by an unusually long and forked tail, providing mastery of both effortless and highly active flight. Few raptors can equal the snatching skill of these kites. Unlike *Elanus*, the *Milvus* kites have developed social behaviour in response to the finding and exploitation of carrion sources and regularly join vultures in such activity. Their nests are built mainly in trees; they lay two or three eggs and raise young whose first plumages are little different from their own. Both kites are migratory in northern latitudes. Europe holds both species, the Red Kite and the Black Kite, but the latter has other populations throughout most of the Old World.

Genus *Haliaeetus* This genus is considered to include fairly primitive raptors, closely related to the last. It is the first group of eagles, usually described as 'fish eagles', and includes at least eight species. They occupy aquatic or maritime habitats throughout almost the entire world and there they hunt or scavenge on aquatic prey, often as large as hares and salmon. To capture such prey they have developed relatively low hunting flight and accurate snatching and plunging techniques at its end. Their wings are broad, enabling them to maintain their lift at slow speed. Thus compared to other eagles (see for example *Aquila*), their form is distinctly vulturine (see for example the *Gyps* vultures) and their similarity to carrion-eating raptors is heightened by their huge, deep bills and large feet. Slow to mature, they may take several years even to attempt breeding. Their nests are usually placed on cliffs or in trees. They normally lay two eggs and raise young in which the final adult plumage is much obscured. As a group, they are less migratory than many other raptors, but extreme winter conditions which lock up food supplies are avoided. In Europe, these mighty birds are represented by the White-tailed Eagle.

Genus *Gypaetus* This genus contains a single, large, vulturine raptor, once called the Bearded

Vulture but now usually known as the Lammergeier. It inhabits montane wildernesses and nearby plains, where it combines carrion-eating with the hunting of live or dying animals. To secure the latter, it will follow the flocks of pastoral man. Unlike the more typical vultures, the Lammergeier is at ease at all levels of air space and its huge, falcon-like form particularly allows the quartering of steppe. Unlike most other vultures, the Lammergeier is a beautiful, colourful raptor with a fully feathered head and neck. The so-called 'beard' is better described as thick whiskers which spray downwards at the base of the beak. The Lammergeier prefers to nest in small caves and usually raises only one young with much duller plumage. An essentially resident species, it may, however, range over huge distances. Its hold on Europe is now slim.

Genus *Neophron* This is another single-species genus, though some systematists combine it with *Necrosyrtes* (see p. 28). Both stem from the more open savannas of Africa where they have developed markedly varied feeding methods. The English name for *Neophron*, the Egyptian Vulture, implies a restricted distribution but it actually inhabits most of the lower northern latitudes of the Old World. There, unusually among accipitrid raptors, the adult is a mainly white bird; unlike other European vultures, it has a fine beak and a nimble gait. It nests in recesses, lays two eggs and raises dark plumaged young. The northernmost communities of the Egyptian Vulture are highly migratory, withdrawing south to Africa, Arabia, and India. Each year fewer return to Europe.

Genus *Gyps* This genus includes six species of huge vultures. They inhabit wildernesses harbouring large mammal populations and within such habitat they have become adapted to a diet of carrion. To find the (currently fast-diminishing) supply of such, they make aerial searches of huge areas. Accordingly their form is adapted to sustained, soaring, and gliding flight—hence their long, broad wings. Their dietary adaptations are most evident in heavy, tearing beaks, bare or thinly feathered heads and necks (to allow easy entry to abdominal cavities), strong legs (to assist tearing), and rather flat talons. The

provision of these features is not equal and there is a marked, specific hierarchy within vultures and over all other scavenging raptors. Lengthy immaturities of at least five years and long fledgling periods of up to three months make breeding a slow process for vultures. As most lay only one egg in their cliff or tree nests, productivity is low. In Europe the genus is represented only by the Griffon Vulture.

Genus *Aegypius* This is another single-species genus, though some systematists do not split it from *Torgos* (see p. 28). Both inhabit the arid wildernesses that attract other vultures, *Aegypius* in southern Eurasia and *Torgos* in the open lands of Africa and Israel. Their form is similar to *Gyps* but only their heads are as bare. Their beaks are, however, massive and their ability to open carcasses thus enhanced. Both choose tree nests and their reproduction is as slow and hazardous as that of *Gyps*. They wear basically uniform, dark plumages at all ages, quite unlike the markedly two-toned dress of *Gyps*. In Europe, only the Black Vulture in this genus occurs.

Genus *Circaetus* This genus contains the snake-eating eagles, of which at least four species are recognized. They are largely confined to African savannas where they have specialized in the hunting of reptiles. To this end, they have developed broad, owl-like faces, flight configurations allowing several modes of hunting which include ponderous hovering, and the unfeathered long legs and short talons required for safely holding down writhing prey. Their bills are relatively smaller than those of mammal-eating raptors. The snake-eagles build their nests on the tops of bushy trees, lay one egg and raise young with plumage almost identical to their own. They begin to breed at three or four years. The single European representative, the Short-toed Eagle, is highly migratory and winters in Africa.

Genus *Circus* This genus includes the less primitive raptors called harriers, of which at least nine species are recognized. They range through all the major continents and inhabit areas of ground cover, both wet and dry. Their general structure is one of the most striking of all raptor groups, since their medium-sized forms contain owl-like faces, slim bodies, long legs, long, flexible wings, and long, often fanned tails. The last two features allow sustained hunting at surface level, and the first three clearly assist the location and capture of prey in dense vegetation. Their appearance is also made striking by the marked sexual difference in adult plumages, with the mainly grey and white males among the most beautiful birds of prey. They feed mainly on ground prey, and they have developed greeting and food-passing flight actions during breeding which are more obvious than in any other group of raptors. In all but one species, their nests are made on the ground or on a mat of reeds. In these, they lay a relatively large number of eggs (up to 12) and rear young which at first resemble their mothers. Most harriers are migratory but not all leave for the African and Asian tropics in winter. In Europe, this attractive group is represented by the Marsh, Hen, Montagu's and Pallid Harriers.

Genus *Melierax* This genus includes the so-called 'chanting goshawks', of which up to four species are recognized. They are essentially African birds, requiring trees for breeding but open savanna for hunting. They have adapted to catching prey on the ground and have long legs and a fast run for this purpose. Otherwise their form and behaviour are not unlike *Accipiter* (see below) except for distinctly rounded tails. They do not however, exhibit sexual dimorphism in their plumage, which resembles that of harrier *Circus* males in the adult and buzzards *Buteo* or honey buzzards *Pernis* in the juvenile. The chanting goshawks build nests deep inside thorn trees and lay only one or two eggs. Their chanting calls are actually better described as multisyllabic, fluting whistles, often uttered for long periods. In the West Palearctic, the genus is represented by the Dark Chanting Goshawk which occurs only in central Morocco. Little is known of this isolated population, but one bird has wandered to Spain.

Genus *Accipiter* At least 42 species are recognized in this largest, most radiated genus of hawks. They range through all the major continents and many adjacent archipelagos and islands, inhabiting mainly wooded and bushy areas. Their general structure is striking since their small to large forms contain vicious beaks,

rather rounded heads, quite long but well rounded bodies, long legs, relatively broad but not long wings, and long, often fanned tails. The last two features allow powerful and highly agile flight, which the hawks use to chase and snatch prey in or from the air. They predate a wide variety of animals and some species have the name 'bird-hawk' attached to them due to their predilection for avian prey. Their appearance varies relatively little, since nearly all have dark upperparts and pale, usually barred underparts. These hawks nest in trees, often using the nests of other tree-nesting species as foundations for their own. Most lay three to five eggs and rear young which resemble their mothers, except usually for streaked underparts. With such a wide range of species it is not surprising that migratory and dispersive behaviour varies considerably. It is most marked at higher latitudes. In Europe, these sudden, agile raptors are represented by the Goshawk, the Sparrowhawk, and the Levant Sparrowhawk. In the extreme east of the West Palearctic, the Shikra also occurs.

Genus *Buteo* This genus comprises the 'true' buzzards, of which about 25 species are recognized. They occur in all the regions of the world except Australasia and have adapted to both wooded and open habitats, tolerating also both wet and dry climates. Their general form is distinctive, since their structures include quite broad, rounded heads, full-chested, barrel-shaped bodies, long and broad wings, well feathered legs and full tails. Their wing and tail shape allow sustained soaring and gliding and these modes of flight allow prey to be spotted and long migrations to be achieved. Their appearance is characterized by usually uniform upperparts and distinctly variable underparts; the patterns of the latter change between and within species and show many confusing overlaps. They predate small mammals in the main but are also opportunistic in their food searches. Their nests are made mostly in trees or on cliff-ledges and their clutches are usually of two or three eggs. The young closely resemble the parents. The migrations of buzzards of higher latitude, continental populations are well-marked, being concentrated over straits and coastal mountain ranges. In Europe, this sky-loving group is represented by the Buzzard, the Long-legged Buzzard, and the Rough-legged Buzzard.

Genus *Aquila* This genus includes the 'true' eagles mainly of the Old World, of which eight species are recognized. They range through most of the northern hemisphere and also occur in Africa and Australasia. Their general structure is among the most well known of all raptors; their large forms contain cruel beaks, obvious gapes, frowning eyebrows, baleful eyes, bulky, powerful bodies, strong feathered or 'booted' legs, and powerful feet with huge talons, long, also broad wings, and quite long, full tails. Like buzzards *Buteo* and the other soaring raptors, the true eagles spend much time on the wing in the search for food sources. Generally they are active predators of ground or water prey, but may also scavenge or rob other birds of their kills. Adult eagles are dark birds with very restricted plumage patterns but their juveniles and immatures may be just the opposite. Eagle nests are placed on trees or cliff-ledges and usually contain two eggs. Most eagles in northern latitudes migrate and all are dispersive during their immaturity. In Europe, this majestic tribe is represented by the Lesser Spotted Eagle, the Spotted Eagle, and Imperial Eagle and the Golden Eagle. In the wider area of the West Palearctic, the Tawny and Steppe Eagle and the Verreaux's Eagle also occur.

Genus *Hieraaetus* This genus contains the so-called 'hawk-eagles', of which at least five species are recognized. All are Old World species, occurring in middle latitudes and usually in montane or heavily wooded regions when breeding. In some respects, their structure differs distinctly from that of *Aquila;* their wings are relatively narrower, their tails obviously longer, and their bodies less bulky. Their appearance is also different with variable plumage patterns recalling both buzzards *Buteo* and kites *Milvus* and thus providing confusing overlaps. Plumage progression in the larger species is also complex. Their aquiline character is, however, always evident in their active and agile predation of gamebirds and small mammals, the birds swooping down with great power. Nest-sites vary from trees and ledges to small caves. One or two eggs are laid. All

hawk-eagles are at least dispersive. In Europe, they are represented by the Booted Eagle (a confusing name also applied generally to *Aquila* eagles) and the Bonelli's Eagle.

Family Pandionidae

Genus *Pandion* This family and genus contain one species; it is the Osprey, the most specialized of all Old World raptors that hunts fish and is often called the 'Fish-hawk'. Its systematics are much argued but currently it is regarded as an accipitrid raptor, even though its modified structure contains a small, narrow head, a compact oily plumage, rather owl-like feet with a reversible outer toe and strongly curved talons, and extremely flexible wings. All these are clearly related to the Osprey's ability to dive on, capture, and fly away with large fish. The Osprey is a markedly widespread raptor, breeding in marine and aquatic habitats throughout the northern hemisphere and Australasia and making its nest usually on top of trees, cliffs, and pinnacles; in parts of North America they have taken readily to man-made sites. It lays three eggs normally and rears young which wear dark upperparts and predominantly white underparts like their parents. In Europe and most of the Holarctic, the Osprey is a summer visitor.

Order FALCONIFORMES

Family Falconidae

Containing the falcons, differing from accipitrid hawks particularly in not building nests (in *Falco*), in killing prey by neck severance, in several structural features, notably a fused spine (in the thorax), false teeth on each cutting edge of the upper mandible (and a corresponding notch on the lower), and two additional bones supporting the musculature of the tail, and in the direction of wing moult.

Genus *Falco* This last genus of the diurnal raptors includes about 40 species which almost match the radiation of *Accipiter* and, like that group, range almost throughout the entire world. Unlike *Accipiter*, the falcons present more distinct integral subgroups, notably the ten kestrels, the ten Hobby-like species, and the ten large falcons. Their general structure is most typified by rather square but not frowning heads, short necks, strong bodies, long and pointed wings, and quite long to long, relatively narrow tails. All these features accommodate powerful chasing or diving flights after flying or running prey, ending in strike and only much modified in the hovering regularly adopted by kestrels and some other species to espy prey prior to capture. They feed on a wide variety of animals and insects. Their appearance varies considerably. Though most species show a contrasting plumage pattern with dark upperparts and pale underparts, others may be wholly dark or mainly white, and marked sexual and juvenile differences occur throughout the genus. The kestrels and some of the other small falcons are colourful. Most falcons prefer to use either holes or old nests for breeding and their clutches usually contain two to five eggs. In Europe, this group is represented by the Lesser Kestrel, the well known Kestrel, the Red-footed Falcon, the Merlin, the Hobby, the Eleonora's Falcon, the Lanner, the Saker, the Gyrfalcon, and the Peregrine. Three other species, the American Kestrel, the Sooty Falcon, and the Barbary Falcon, also occur in the West Palearctic.

EVOLUTION

Birds stem from reptile-like ancestors and are apparent in the fossil record from the Jurassic period. Predatory forms are visible in the Cretaceous period, but the first evidence of a generalized bird of prey did not appear until the Eocene period. This was the time, from 65 to 75 million years ago, when the major evolution of the world's avifauna probably took place. Among the 27 modern bird families identifiable in the Eocene period are the vultures, the hawks, and the owls. By the Miocene period 25 million years ago, the falcons also appear; and by the Pliocene, 10 million years ago, it is likely that the diversity of raptors was at its greatest as part of the probable maximum radiation of all bird species. The repeated glaciations of the Pleistocene period, beginning about one million years ago, then took their toll, enforcing dispersals and causing extinctions. In the current inter-glacial epoch, the so-called Holocene period, losses continued, mainly at the hand of man. Thus of the 290 extant birds of prey (making up about 3 per cent of 9000 or so

avian species left alive after the Pleistocene), perhaps only one in ten species is not at risk. In the 300 years since the last Dodo died, one island raptor has gone and three others are in great peril.

The chances of an increased radiation of raptorial species are now slim, though the potential for such is still evident in the relatively recent and local development of races (sub-species). In the West Palearctic, at least 13 species have differing island, peninsular, and continental forms and 12 of these (radiating from 10 species) are visible in Europe. Perhaps the best examples are found in the Goshawk, which has, in addition to the widespread nominate race, a relatively large, pale form in the northern taiga and a relatively small and dark form confined to Corsica and Sardinia. In addition, the small, pink-bodied Peregrine of Iberia may be mentioned, but to do so brings in the constant taxonomic vexations that the raptor systematist has to face, for this bird is clearly closely related to the Barbary Falcon. Probably the worst confusion of this kind surrounds the Tawny and Steppe Eagle (or Eagles) but most European observers are spared the problem of separating them.

Unlike the major avian group of ducks, geese, and swans that precede them systematically, the diurnal birds of prey present no tendency to genetic looseness. Hybridization between their species and tribes is virtually unknown.

HABITAT

The diurnal raptors have a world-wide distribution (except for Antarctica), occurring as predators and scavengers in all the great regional faunas and in a variety of climatic zones and habitats. The majority of species are essentially arboreal or rock-loving and wherever there are land features that allow soaring flight, many birds may use them. One major habitat that has not been fully utilized is the coastline. Although the White-tailed Eagle, the Gyr Falcon, and the Peregrine freely hunt marine birds, and other species such as the Eleonora's Falcon especially kill sea-crossing, migrant landbirds, no diurnal raptor has primarily evolved as a marine predator. The vacancy in such a role has been taken by species in three other avian Orders, most con-

Table 1 Habitat preferences of diurnal raptors breeding in Europe

	Tundra	Taiga	Temperate moors, marshes, and mountains	Temperate woodland	Temperate or sub-tropical steppe	Sub-tropical, semi-arid woodland and mountains	Deserts and semi-deserts	Aquatic habitats	Towns	No. of habitat types occupied
Honey Buzzard				*						1
Black-winged Kite					*					1
Black Kite				*	*	*			*	4
Red Kite				*		*				2
White-tailed Eagle								*		1
Lammergeier						*				1
Egyptian Vulture					*	*	*		*	4
Griffon Vulture						*	*			2
Black Vulture						*	*			2
Short-toed Eagle					*		*			2
Marsh Harrier			*					*		2
Hen Harrier		†	*							1–2
Pallid Harrier					*					1
Montagu's Harrier			*		*					2
Goshawk		*		*		*				3
Sparrowhawk		†		*		*				2–3
Levant Sparrowhawk						*				1
Buzzard		*	*	*		*				4
Long-legged Buzzard						*	*			2
Rough-legged Buzzard	*	*								2
Lesser Spotted Eagle				*						1
Spotted Eagle				*						1
Imperial Eagle						*				1
Golden Eagle	*	*	*			*	*			5
Booted Eagle						*				1
Bonelli's Eagle						*	*			2
Osprey								*		1
Lesser Kestrel					*	*			*	3
Kestrel			*		*	*	*		*	5
Red-Footed Falcon				*	*					2
Merlin		*	*		*					3
Hobby				*		*				2
Eleonora's Falcon								*		1
Lanner					*	*	*			3
Saker						*				1
Gyrfalcon	*	*								2
Peregrine	*	*	*		*	*	*		*	7
Total no. of raptors using habitat type	4	7–9	8	10	12	21	10	4	5	37

* Occurs regularly; † occurs occasionally or locally.

vergently by the hawk-like skuas. Throughout the world, the birds of prey occur in 12 major habitat types. For the European species, indications of their marked habitat preferences have already been given and an attempt follows to display them systematically. Seen from Table 1, the habitats that support the greatest diversity of raptors are subtropical, semi-arid woodlands and mountains. Regions of such character are restricted to the southern extremities of Europe and the would-be student must visit Spain and Greece to see the fullest range of European raptors. Few other countries retain sufficient undisturbed habitats to support both diverse and populous communities of diurnal raptors, though those with large taiga tracts have probably the most secure ones. The right-hand column in Table 1 demonstrates the high degree of habitat specialization: one in three of the European species occupies only one main habitat and a second one in three occurs in only two. Only seven diurnal raptors (the Black Kite, the Egyptian Vulture, the Buzzard, the Golden Eagle, the Kestrel, the Lanner, and the Peregrine) show anything approaching the wide habitat tolerances of the common passerines; and of these, only the Kestrel (along with its nocturnal companion, the Tawny Owl) has made a success of urban life and, increasingly, the land-littoral ribbons of road edges. In generic and familial terms, the most adaptive group is that of the falcons which occur in all nine habitats, followed by the 'true' eagles in seven and their close relatives, the buzzards, in six. This situation has led to the supposition that these birds are less primitive than the rest of the accipitrid hawks and vultures but such views, even if well-founded, cannot detract from the high degree of ecological specialization or acquired skill in those species, particularly obvious in the wasp-larvae-eating Honey Buzzard, the bone-dropping Lammergeier, the snake-hunting Short-toed Eagle, and the fish-catching Osprey.

DISTRIBUTION, NUMBERS, AND MORTALITY

As indicated in the Foreword, the chief controls upon the present numbers and distribution of the diurnal birds of prey have been the direct and indirect onslaughts of man. Of these, the oldest and most continuous have been the destruction of natural habitats to make way for intensive agriculture, and the killing of suspect predators to protect increasingly valuable stock and game. By the late nineteenth century, the numbers of some raptors were so much reduced that their scarcity increased their value as trophies and the resultant trade in stuffed specimens, eggs, and falconer's birds became a significant factor in local extinctions. Although today the Osprey shows every sign of recovering its former ground in northern Britain, it should never be forgotten that it was hounded to extinction in the same area only 90 years ago.

The tide of the onslaughts against raptors has partly turned in the twentieth century, with the accidental combination of reduced game management in the two world wars and improved understanding (and increased protection) allowing first breathing spaces and second a few safe havens. Unfortunately, the next changes were entirely detrimental; in the middle of this century, the ecosystems of all European countries were more or less tainted by a flood of agricultural chemicals, many of which proved to be persistent as well as poisonous. They affected the vital food chains of higher animals to a point where many became nothing short of lethal and among the widespread collapses of populations that followed, those of raptors were often prominent. Memories cloud quickly but only 15–20 years ago,

even the widespread Sparrowhawk, as well as rarer species such as the Peregrine and Golden Eagle, were at risk in Britain. There and elsewhere in Europe, where conservationists have won the battles against pesticide misuse and for habitat preservation, some common raptors are back from the brink but most birds of prey are continuing to decline. Inevitably, therefore, their distribution in Europe and the West Palearctic is subject to continuing change. Considered against those that could have been supported by the natural climax habitats of post-glacial Europe, the current ranges and populations of diurnal raptors are thought to be respectively more restricted and less dense. Certainly about a third of the species appear to have the potential to occupy more ground. It is sometimes, however, extremely difficult to prove any overall trends in distribution shifts and population densities. The secretive nature of most breeding raptors and the variations of their migratory behaviour cloud the view of even the most adventurous analyst. Few national ornithologies contain numerical histories and among those that do exist, succeeding estimates vary widely. Thus of the 39 species breeding or attempting to breed in Europe, the information for five is too limited to allow any conclusion, for three suggestive of no marked change, for five indicative of locally differing trends (featuring both increases and decreases), and for 26 sufficient to demonstrate clear, often marked declines and range contractions.

The most stable species are the Honey Buzzard, the Pallid Harrier (of marginal occurrence in Europe), and the Rough-legged Buzzard (of northerly occurrence and subject to short-term fluctuations caused by prey densities). The locally successful species are the Black Kite (particularly in central and western regions), the Hen Harrier, the Buzzard (in spite of the added scourge of epidemic disease in the rabbit), the Golden Eagle (due to protection), the Booted Eagle (in eastern regions), the Sparrowhawk and the Kestrel (in some areas now cleansed of toxic chemicals), the Hobby (in oddly scattered regions), the Saker (in north-east areas), and now the Peregrine (in some western maritime regions). The most threatened species are the vultures, the Imperial Eagle (with both races now greatly reduced), the Montagu's Harrier (suffering a widespread and unexplained decline), the Lesser Kestrel (recently much decreased even in its strongholds), the Gyrfalcon (subject to excessive persecution and perhaps climatic change), and the Lanner (now brought close to European extinction by persecution and exploitation). Of the last group, the vultures face a particularly bleak future, for reasons already given in the notes on their classification.

In terms of relative abundance, the most common diurnal bird of prey is undoubtedly the Kestrel. It may well outnumber any other by two to one and provide two-fifths of the total raptor population of Europe. Apparently second is the Buzzard, followed by the Sparrowhawk, the Lesser Kestrel, the Black Kite, the Hobby, the Goshawk, and the Honey Buzzard. Where numerical estimates of European raptor populations exist, they are given in the texts opposite the plates portraying perched birds. Many species have retained strongholds, either in areas of remaining preferred habitats or in those with effective conservation, and these regions are quickly demonstrated by an overlay of the rapidly improving maps of breeding distribution of which the most accurate are found in *The Birds of the Western Palearctic*. Judged by the estimates of populations given in that work, the European strongholds of raptors number five and their rough order of numerical importance appears to be Iberia (holding 25 species), Poland and European Russia (25), south-east Europe (28), and Britain (14). Between these regions, other areas still do support wide diversities of raptors (with, for example, 18 species in France) but their populations are clearly pocketed by habitat restriction and disturbance and appear to be less numerous. In contrast to the stronghold populations, the small local or thinly scattered communities of the rarest raptors (not included in above totals) stand out starkly. Of these, the most precious accipitrid species are the Black-winged Kites of Portugal and Spain, the Lammergeiers of Greece, the Pyrénées, and Corsica, the Long-legged Buzzards of the Balkans, and the Imperial Eagles of Spain and the Balkans. In the falcons, three species have to be similarly valued. They are the Red-footed Falcons of eastern Europe, the Eleonora's Falcon whose entire world population lies along an arc from the Canary Islands through the Mediterranean to Cyprus, and the

Lanners, now reduced to a few last nest sites in the central and eastern Mediterranean.

MOVEMENTS

In order to exploit their maximal breeding habitats and summer food sources, most of the diurnal raptors of Europe and the West Palearctic undertake long and often dramatic migrations, while even the large sedentary species may disperse during the long years of their immaturity. The degrees of such behaviour and the distances overflown before a winter home is reached may vary by latitude and longitude and also within species. The severe polar or continental climate of northern and eastern Europe forces migration upon nearly all diurnal raptors; the more maritime regime of western Europe allows residency for some; and the warmth of certain Mediterranean pockets permits many to linger in some winters. Generally, however, large areas of Europe see two vast migrations every year, northbound in the spring and southbound in the autumn. Because of the marked reluctance of the broad-winged soaring species to cross the open sea, their movements are markedly concentrated along leading mountain ranges (with a regular supply of uplifting air), over peninsulas, near sea coasts, and across straits. In Europe there are four classic stations for the observation of migrating raptors: Falsterbo at the southern point of Sweden, the Straits of Gibraltar (where the Rock and the crags of Ceuta form an impressive backcloth to their passage), across the Sicilian channel, and the area of the Bosporus.

At such places, up to 12 soaring species of raptors can be seen in day-long passage on both spring and autumn migrations. The latter have been increasingly monitored in the last 30 years and although there are some puzzling discrepancies, the autumn passages over Gibraltar and the Bosporus can be roughly scaled at 200 000 and 100 000 birds respectively. Some east European birds travel south beyond the Black Sea and their autumn numbers and those of their near Asian relatives are apparently even larger, at probably some 350 000. The return passages have been less fully quantified but it is now known that up to 600 000 diurnal raptors pass north along the western side of the Gulf of Aqaba in spring and eventually disperse into Europe and Asia. Observations on this last movement in 1977 produced staggering counts of 226 000 Honey Buzzards and 316 000 Buzzards. By comparison with these, movements elsewhere in Europe and the Middle East are small. The autumn exodus of about 10 000 Honey Buzzards and 17 000 Buzzards from Falsterbo remains the most marked in western Europe. In contrast to the soaring species, some of the smaller hawks and all the falcons use their more active flight to cross both land and sea directly and their passages are essentially broad-front and little observed, except in the case of the spring return across north-east Africa.

Of the 37 West Palearctic diurnal raptors that breed in Europe, 23 winter in Africa. Their movements therein are not all defined and their final distributions do not always match the main longitudes of the breeding ranges. In many winter ranges, the tropical rain forest belt appears unattractive and the main destinations for the long-distance migrants are the trans-continental, drier savannas south of the Sahara and the continuation of this habitat down the eastern side of the continent. The whole or most of these areas are freely exploited by all the harriers, the Black Kite, the Lesser Kestrel, and the Kestrel, but the other species are noticeably more scattered or localized, for example the Red-footed Falcon which ends up in south-west Africa and the Eleonora's Falcon which crosses over the path of the former to winter mainly in Madagascar. Within their winter grounds, European raptors are not always sedentary; in particular, the insectivorous species constantly shift to exploit the prey sources occasioned by rain and may have accomplished two-thirds of their northward return by February. Of all the species, the most distant travellers are the Hobby and the Red-footed Falcon, of which some may annually pass through 90° of latitude and whose main winter ranges are in the southern third of Africa.

FOOD

Without some red meat in their bills, the images of the birds of prey seem incomplete to many. In reality, however, their diet is somewhat different, for while the majority do consume warm-blooded flesh, many readily take a wide variety of other animal foods and some specialize on very few organisms. The total range of prey types includes mammals, birds, reptiles, amphibians, fish, invertebrates, and even vegetable matter and organic waste. Most members of the accipitrid family earn their living wholly by predation, but others may combine predation with scavenging, and others specialize in carrion-eating. These variations in dietary behaviour may be exemplified respectively by first the dashing Sparrowhawk or the powerful Golden Eagle, second the elegant Red Kite and the rather sluggish Tawny Eagle, and third any of the typical vultures. The size and power of the species correlates with the size of prey and the method of hunting and feeding. The ranges of prey sizes and food sources are wide, from tiny termites to full-grown African elephants. Most powerful raptors can kill prey of several times their own weight, but usually they predate animals of about half their weight. In those species whose sexes differ markedly in size, such as the accipitrid hawks, the prey of the larger female is bulkier and less diverse than that of the smaller male.

As already indicated, most raptors kill various prey and even those with names or reputations that imply a strict diet, like the Sparrowhawk and the Honey Buzzard, take more types of food than might be expected. Table 2 sets out the so far recognized prey types and food sources of the diurnal raptors that breed in Europe. Of the ten food classes analysed, only one species, the Black Kite, takes from them all. Otherwise, as genera, the true kites, the harriers, the buzzards, and the true eagles are noticeably more flexible in diet than the accipitrid hawks, the Booted, and Bonelli's Eagles, the falcons, and the large vultures. The most restricted diets are shown by the Sparrowhawk, the Booted Eagle, the Merlin, and the Eleonora's Falcon; all of these take a high proportion of birds, which just exceed mammals in the overall record of raptorial diet. Insects are important to only three of the accipitrid species but form a major part of the diet of four of the ten falcons. Reptiles feature markedly among the food of the accipitrid species of arid regions. Frequent fish-catching requires unusual skills and in Europe, only three species—the Black Kite, the White-tailed Eagle, and above all the Osprey—

	Mammals	Birds	Insects	Reptiles	Amphibians	Fish	Other inverte-brates	Carrion	Vegetable matter and organic waste	No. of types eaten
33 predominantly hunting species										
Honey Buzzard	†	†	*	†	†		†		†	7
Black-winged Kite	*	*	†	†						4
Black Kite	*	*	†	†	†	*	†	*	†	9
Red Kite	*	*	†	†	†	†	†	†	†	9
White-tailed Eagle	†	*		†	†	*		†		6
Short-toed Eagle	†	†	†	*	†		†			6
Marsh Harrier	*	*	†	†	†	†	†	†		8
Hen Harrier	*	*	†	†	†	†		†		7
Pallid Harrier	*	*	†	†						4
Montagu's Harrier	*	*	†	†	†					5
Goshawk	*	*	†					†		4
Sparrowhawk	†	*	†							3
Levant Sparrowhawk	†	†	*	*						4
Buzzard	*	†	†	†	†	†	†	†		8
Long-legged Buzzard	*	†	*	*						4
Rough-legged Buzzard	*	†	†		†	†				5
Lesser Spotted Eagle	*	†	†	†	†					5
Spotted Eagle	*	†	†	†	†	†		†		7
Imperial Eagle	*	†	†	†		†		†		6
Golden Eagle	*	*	†	†	†	†		†		7
Booted Eagle	†	*		*						3
Bonelli's Eagle	*	*		†				†		4
Osprey	†	†	†	†	†	*				6
Lesser Kestrel	†	†	*	†	†					5
Kestrel	*	†	†	†			†		†	6
Red-footed Falcon	†	†	*	†	†					5
Merlin	†	*	†							3
Hobby	†	*	*	†						4
Eleonora's Falcon		*	*							2
Lanner	†	*	†	†	†					5
Saker	*	†	†	†	†					5
Gyrfalcon	†	*	†		†	†				5
Peregrine	†	*	†	†	†			†		6
Total no. of species eating prey types frequently/occasionally	18/14	19/14	7/23	4/23	0/20	3/9	0/7	1/11	0/4	
4 predominantly scavenging species										
Lammergeier	*	†		†						3
Egyptian Vulture	*	†	†	†	†	†	†	most prey	†	8
Griffon Vulture	*	†				†		consumed in		3
Black Vulture	*	†		†		†		this state	†	5
Total no. of species utilizing food sources frequently/occasionally	4/0	0/4	0/1	0/3	0/1	0/3	0/1	4/0	0/2	
Total no. of species consuming	36	37	31	30	21	15	8	16	5	

* Major part of diet; † minor or irregular part of diet.

have these. Dietary opportunism is widely displayed, but only three diurnal raptors—the Black Kite, the Red Kite, and the Egyptian Vulture—have been able to exploit the food waste of man. Vegetable matter is, not surprisingly, ignored by the vast majority of species.

The variety of diet in diurnal raptors is accompanied by a wide range of hunting techniques. Most accipitrid species catch their prey on the ground, or sometimes from water surfaces, and do so either from flight or a hunting perch, their final act being a powerful pounce. Some of the swifter flying species catch their prey in the air, after either a searching and flushing flight or a lunge from a hunting perch. The small hawks of the genus *Accipiter* are the most skilled at this mode, but even large eagles of the genus *Aquila* can employ it. Some accipitrid species indulge in the piracy of their fellows' food. In this respect, the Black Kite shows once again its all-purpose role as a raptor chasing birds as daunting as the White-tailed Eagle and even stealing directly from man.

How precisely prey die during their final capture by accipitrid species is inadequately known but clearly death is caused by one, some or all of the following: the shock of the pounce, the grip of the feet, and the incision of the talons. Apparently, however, accipitrid species do not often deliver the nuchal *coup de grâce* with the bill that is characteristic of the falcons. Further information on feeding actions is given in the account of daily cycles in the next section.

In contrast to most accipitrid species which show considerable opportunism in their diet, the falcons are highly predatory and, in Europe, only one (rarely) exploits carrion. The bird-hunting species typically take their prey by stooping upon it at great speed, either striking it out of the sky or gripping it and forcing it down, or gripping it and taking it directly to a perch. In this mode, the best example is the fearsome stoop of the Peregrine on a pigeon. A few falcons, such as the Lanner and the Saker, will also stoop on prey on the ground and others, most notably the Merlin, typically outfly their prey to seize them at the end of a relatively level, however variably directed, chase. The most elegant species, such as the Hobby and the Eleonora's Falcon, are able to stoop, chase, and also idle in the upper airspace, snatching passing birds and insects. Hovering prior to pouncing is the classic behaviour of the mainly mammal-consuming Kestrel, but both it and its close relatives freely adopt other techniques, such as the flushing flight of the Sparrowhawk and aerial insect-catching. If not killed outright by the raking hind claw of a stooping bird, the captured prey of falcons are often dispatched by the severance of the neck spine through a nip from their powerful bills. In contrast to the accipitrid species falcons are only casually piratical. The smaller falcons may congregate to exploit localized prey such as swarming insects.

None of the comments in the last two paragraphs applies strictly to the vultures. With the exception of the Lammergeier which directly attacks weakened animals (with wing-beating rather than claw or bill strikes) on occasion, all are innocent of the deaths that provide animal food sources to them. Thus their hunting is typically composed of long, solitary aerial searches and much shorter, social feeding. The vultures are adept at picking up every clue to the presence of carrion. It is rare for one to have a feast to itself. Generally, large carcasses are opened via the softest external tissues and the viscera are consumed first. The smallest European species, the Egyptian Vulture, shows considerable dietary adaptability (and, in some African populations, it has learnt to use stones to break eggs). It may also break bones to extract marrow, but that habit is the forte of the Lammergeier.

As a result of their diet, all the raptors have to face the risk of swallowing indigestible material and all take considerable care in the final acts of feeding, plucking their large prey and avoiding its major bones before ingestion. Feathers, hair, and horny parts are, however, frequently taken in and these are regurgitated as pellets. Skulls and bones are more frequently visible in the pellets of the accipitrid species than in those of the falcons. A particular display associated with feeding is that called mantling, during which the bird provides a canopy for its prey by spreading its wings and threatens any potential pirate.

The winter diets of diurnal raptors may alter little or a lot. An example of marked change occurs in the Lesser Kestrel, the Hobby, and the Red-footed Falcon, which become almost completely insectivorous in central and southern Africa, exploiting particularly the rain-induced emergences of termites. Winter opportunism also shows in the large raptors, with, for example, the Marsh Harrier often hunting ground prey well away from aquatic habitat and the migrant Steppe Eagle being another bird to exploit termites, even hunting them on foot in flocks.

SOCIAL PATTERN AND BEHAVIOUR

Nearly all active predators hunt alone. This is not to say that they do so at random, since most use fixed feeding ranges in both summer and winter and may take up such on migration. Some active predators may join together to exploit areas of unusually concentrated food supplies and within these a few, such as the kites, the harriers, the kestrels, and the Rough-legged Buzzard, share with some owls the habit of communal roosting. In general, however, the only European raptors that behave socially throughout the year are the specialized scavengers and the insectivorous falcons. In their case, the advantages of shared food searches are obvious and have led to interdependence between both individuals of a species and a variety of species. The solitariness of raptors is, of course, reduced by pair-formation in the breeding season, but not to any marked extent. The dispersion of adult pairs within a breeding habitat is usually wide and generally only small nesting territories are defended within larger, often overlapping home ranges. Most of the exceptions to these rules relate to feeding behaviour, both normal and opportunistic, and include more or less colonial nesting by the kites, some vultures, the harriers, and some small insectivorous falcons. It is, however, rare for such associations to be visible in Europe except in countries adjoining the Mediterranean.

The birds of prey are typically monogamists. In the larger, primarily sedentary species, the pair-bond may be life-long and demonstrated by year-through association but in most species, it breaks down after the breeding season, is lost on migration and in winter ranges and is taken up again only during the reoccupation of breeding sites. It is during the last-mentioned state of annual behaviour that the majority of raptors are found most easily and observed; then they advertise their presence by calling and performing distinctive aerial displays within and over their territories. Many of the flight actions have generic and even specific characters, treated in detail and often illustrated in *The Birds of the Western Palearctic*, and they include high circles, fast winnowing patrols, dramatic sky-dances and, even more exciting, mutual aerobatics involving both members of a pair. The last category includes the famous food-pass most developed in the harriers and lasting throughout the breeding season. The displays of perched raptors have been less well studied but several common postures are known. Perhaps the best observed and certainly the most traditional is the threat post-

ure, in which the bird erects its head and neck feathers, stretches its head upwards or forwards and opens its wings in the 'spread-eagle' attitude; this is the posture adopted for heraldic use by humans. Its effect is to enhance the bird's apparent power and ferocity and to allow a strike from its cleared and extended talons. The threat posture is innate, being adopted by nestlings who will even lie on their backs and strike upwards with their talons. Most threat displays are associated with nest or individual disturbance, but they also assist social raptors to secure an early place in food queues. Flight may inhibit the ability of birds of prey to threaten others, but some species have developed a head-up attitude which clearly echoes the perched posture. Another intruder reaction shown by breeding raptors is the remarkable body flattening of adult and feathered nestlings in the nest; this appears to be stimulated only by the approach of man. Both adult and young birds of prey have a bent-legged, level-backed greeting and solicitation posture. In it the head is held low and calling is often continuous. Variations to this include the head-bowed, upright stance shared by both members of a pair of falcons when food is presented at the nest, and the head-bowed, drooped-winged attitude adopted by females ready to accept copulation.

As the diurnal raptors start breeding, they become more secretive. Final courtship and mating occur on or close to the newly built or refurbished nest and, once eggs are laid, the females of many species take up the whole duty of incubation while their mates devote their time to hunting for both. Since male raptors are generally smaller and shyer than their mates, this division of roles tends to increase their invisibility particularly in wooded habitats and is one factor that makes the assessment of their populations difficult. Within the families of European raptors, there are several exceptions to these comments. Those species with modes of high flight that relate to normal hunting behaviour are more or less constantly visible in fine weather. Thus the vultures, the soaring buzzards and eagles, and the hovering falcons are much easier to detect than the harriers and the low-flying hawks. During the latter part of the breeding season, the demands of growing young take up even more time and raptors are usually at their least visible in late summer and early autumn. Thereafter there is often a marked flush of fledged young and of worn adults. The reappearance is short-lived, however, for dispersal and migration soon cause shifts and withdrawals in most species.

One important point about the behaviour of raptors not brought out above is the regularity of their daily cycle of activity. Whether roosting at a favoured spot in their non-breeding range or near the nest, most raptors begin the day by preening, casting pellets of indigestible material, and defecating. Some may also call, particularly during the early part of the breeding season. Their next acts depend much upon their hunting method, with those species which search for prey from low-level flight or a vantage point generally on the wing before those which habitually soar. Thus the smaller species flit from hunting perch to hunting perch or begin their hovering, and the larger ones launch into a wide survey of prey- or carrion-bearing habitat. The amount of time spent on hunting by raptors has been much debated. Clearly insectivorous species require more time than the carnivores and all increase their efforts when feeding young. Many raptors are best known as distant perched silhouettes and their days clearly contain much loafing. Normal hunting behaviour is inhibited by rain and low cloud but only prolonged adverse climatic conditions, such as deep snow, appear to have a serious effect on killing rates.

Once a raptor has made a successful strike and killed its prey, either by general force, grip, or a nip through the neck, it has to prepare it for ingestion. The removal or parting of indigestible pelage, plumage, or hard parts may be accomplished at the killing point but many species take their smaller victims away to a plucking post. Only the weak-footed vultures cannot do this. The plucking process is remarkably thorough in hawks and buzzards but much less so in falcons, which are often content simply to open the chest of their avian prey. Since feeding for raptors is necessarily a gory business, it might be thought that they would wash and drink after its completion. Surprisingly little evidence exists for the former and even less for the latter.

When not hunting, eating, and loafing, the birds of prey can be seen to indulge in activities that may assist skill training and maintenance, or be a form of 'play'. Such behaviour is most obvious in the soaring of replete vultures and the mock attacks of falcons.

The end of a diurnal raptor's day is variable. As the air cools and thermal activity subsides, the soaring species descend and may go early to their roosts. The more active hunters may, however, exploit the late behaviour of their prey and some, notably the small hawks and falcons, may remain active until dusk, creating havoc among roosting birds and flying insects. Eventually all go to their mainly solitary roosts and sleep in noticeably hunched postures, having passed a day in which perhaps only a quarter to a third of the daylight hours is spent on active behaviour (Brown and Amadon 1968). It is important to remember that most diurnal raptors are fierce and aggressive, with the larger females often clearly dominating their mates, and that this intrinsic behaviour naturally inhibits the keeping of close company.

BREEDING BIOLOGY

Throughout Europe and the West Palearctic, the diurnal raptors are mostly attuned to breeding in spring and summer. The limits of the breeding season may be extended, especially in warmer latitudes and by the larger species, but are restricted in the far north where the summer is brief. The birds build or refurbish nests in a variety of positions in trees, on cliff-ledges, and less commonly in ground cover. Most accipitrid species and the Osprey are active in nest construction, bringing in branches and sticks and filling these in with twigs, rubbish, and finally green foliage and grass. Their nests often become bulky but because they are generally well-hidden and difficult to reach, their detection and predation is not easy. Nest-building and refurbishment is usually undertaken by both sexes, and repairs or decoration with new material may continue during the incubation and fledging periods. The falcons nest in a similar range of situations but use holes and small ledges more commonly than the other hawks. Unlike them, but like the owls, the falcons are not active in nest construction and usually take over old nests of other species or adopt naturally safe egg-holding sites.

The eggs of diurnal raptors are proportionately quite large when compared to those of most other birds. Their shape is usually broadly oval in accipitrid species but more rounded in the falcons. The ground-colour of the eggs is essentially white and the markings are usually shades of red-brown. In general, the eggs of falcons are more intensely blotched and coloured than those of the accipitrid species. The size of egg clutches varies from small to medium; most vultures lay only one egg, most eagles and some buzzards two or three, and the other accipitrid hawks up to six. The Hobby-like falcons lay only two or three, most other small and the large falcons three to five, and the Kestrel up to six eggs. Clutch sizes may vary in response to fluctuations in prey species. Lost clutches are often replaced by the smaller raptors but no European raptor is truly double-brooded. Incubation begins with the first or second egg and takes four to eight weeks, with the larger species usually the slowest to hatch their young. As with most birds, the female hawk or falcon carries out the effective incubation of the eggs. Her mate usually restricts his early nest duties to brief cover of the eggs during her absences. Fledging takes longer than incubation and lasts from four weeks in small species to over four months in the largest. During the early stages, the care and feeding of the nestlings remains the priority of the female but later on, both parents may have to share hunting and nest duties.

All birds of prey make considerable efforts to tend their young, with delicate bill-to-bill feeding a particular feature. Their young, however, are more aggressive, and in the accipitrid raptors, the dominance of the first-hatched young (hence also the first to eat and gather strength) is marked. In some species, the later-hatched nestlings never survive, and all, particularly the smaller males, have to compete fiercely for food and space. The benefit of this 'Cain and Abel' behaviour remains notably unclear. The young of falcons are spared it and their parents are often noticeably attentive to their late developers. Once fledged, the young raptors spend largely unmeasured periods of continuing dependency upon their parents. These may be as short as a fortnight in small species or as long as five months in the largest vultures.

Throughout the breeding season, most diurnal raptors exhibit a bold defence of their nest-site, their aggression being most marked when young are present. Many birds, whatever the species,

may also choose to slip away or demonstrate their concern only at a distance.

The age at which diurnal raptors first breed is variable, though again loosely connected to size. Thus the small hawks, the harriers, and some falcons may pair and raise young within a year or two of their own hatching, most falcons do so in their second year, and the kites and buzzards in their second or third year. For the large eagles and vultures, however, successful pairing and breeding is longer delayed, until the fourth to the ninth year from hatching.

PLUMAGES AND MOULTS

Young diurnal raptors hatch already covered in down, even though they all spend weeks and even months of relative inactivity in the nest. Undoubtedly the down is essentially protective of the individual nestling in nest situations which may suffer from the risks of exposure, competition, and aggression from its fellows, and (in later stages) incomplete brooding by its parents. The down is of two types, one immediate but mostly ephemeral and the other less immediate but lasting throughout the fledging period. The second type is often snow-white and is succeeded by similarly coloured down-like feathers that continue to exist under the successive outer or contour sets of feathers. The first of these is the juvenile plumage which in raptors usually differs most from adult dress in the pale tips and margins of back, wing, and tail-feathers, the heavier marking, usually in the form of streaks, of the underparts, and the closer, narrower bars of the tail. In general, juvenile plumages do not present the sexual differences common in adult raptors, and young birds usually resemble their mothers.

After the assumption of a first full plumage, general rules on its progression are difficult to establish. Fundamentally, plumage changes are related to the age of sexual maturity, which varies from one to nine years and in a rough relationship to size. Thus plumage progression tends to increase in complexity as the size of the species increases. In many of the smaller hawks and falcons, the first change is the replacement of their body and inner wing feathers in their first autumn or within a few months of fledging. The first full change of plumage occurs at about 15 months and the plumage then assumed is identical to that of the adult. In some small falcons, however, and in most larger raptors, there are intermediate, annually replaced plumages that indicate the periods of immaturity by displaying first distinct, but later increasingly adult-like patterns. These are most obvious in the fish- and 'true' eagles. In the latter group, some species—for example the Spotted and Lesser Spotted Eagles—have attracted English names that reflect their immature and not their adult appearance. It should also be noted that plumage progression may vary between individuals as well as between species. Thus ageing by plumage may be a somewhat dubious exercise, however much ornithologists indulge in it.

The moults of birds are still under active study but in the raptors, they show some interesting features. For the larger, soaring accipitrid species, the replacement of the long primary quills of the outer wing is a critical process and many of them have developed an irregular sequence for this, so that there is no chance of a large gap appearing and disturbing the lift in or the balance of their planing surfaces. Interestingly, in some of these species the normal moult direction (from the innermost outwards) is still shown in immature plumages. In contrast, all the falcons have a common moult sequence beginning with the fourth inner primary and proceeding in both directions. No accipitrid hawk shows this and it is another basic distinguishing character between these two orders of diurnal raptors. The whole cycle of moult may take up to six months in small species and up to three years in large ones, with individual feather replacements often incomplete and plumages thus frequently mixed. In migratory species, moult may be delayed until the birds have reached their winter quarters. In more sedentary ones moult is usually a summer event. The nest-bound, female accipitrid hawks moult during the breeding season but their food-providing mates must await its end.

The long primary feathers of the large raptors end in distinctively narrowed vanes. These are frequently referred to as 'fingers' and they exhibit remarkable sensitivity to air currents, being clearly crucial to efficient soaring. The number of notched 'fingers' tends to vary in relation to the incidence of prolonged soaring in the general flight action of a species. Thus, for example, the vultures and the Golden Eagle have more separated primaries than the Spotted Eagle and the broad-winged hawks.

Another obvious plumage adaptation in the diurnal raptors is the loss of feathers around the beak—most developed in the vultures and clearly essentially a sanitary response to their gory diet. Modifications of plumage also occur in the thigh feathers of raptors. These are often unusually long and distinctly coloured and appear to be used in association with changes in wing attitude (and the glaring eyes of many species) in threat and also feeding displays.

Subspecific variation in the diurnal raptors is largely beyond the scope of this book but it should be noted that throughout the world, desert races tend to be pale, humid-area forms dark, while high-arctic morphs tend to white. Individual variation is also marked in birds of prey, with for example more than half the buzzards *Buteo* and Honey Buzzard *Pernis* sporting dark or melanistic variants. Erythristic variants, in which the plumage is drenched chestnut, also occur. Such points should always be kept in mind when an unusually plumaged hawk is seen.

RAPTORS AND MAN

Except in the case of the first falconers, then ornithologists and birdwatchers, and nowadays the growing numbers of converts to conservation, the attitudes of men towards the birds of prey have varied from no more fond than indifferent to usually far more cruel than hostile. The raptor's natural role in animal selection has been seen, through the cloyed vision of sentiment, as excessive and, in an alarming anthropomorphic extension of prejudice, as economically damaging. Particularly in the late eighteenth and nineteenth century their public image became strangely confused, with hints of ancient respect (in heraldic use) overwhelmed by indiscriminate persecution. Proof of needless slaughter abounds in Europe, North America, and Australia and some blame for this must attach to English-speaking sportsmen, whose methods of game management and livestock protection stemmed from various mistaken assumptions and were not amended by observation until well into the twentieth century.

Given the exaggerated faults with which the birds of prey were charged, it is surprising that extinction did not close the lives of many more species than the single Pacific falcon that has disappeared in the last 290 years. What is not surprising is the fact that most diurnal raptors have had their futures put at risk by modern forces even more dangerous than the ignorant gamekeeper's gun or poisoned bait. Ironically, as better understanding of raptorial diet eased the direct execution of the birds of prey, the danger to food chains from persistent chemicals and the increasing pressures of human food production and forestry upon wilderness and marginal agricultural land raised new and possibly terminal threats, not just to species but to whole communities.

Happily the threat posed by the indiscriminate use of toxic chemicals has been largely contained in Europe and most other developed regions. Sadly the risks posed by the wood-consuming industry and by modern, intensive agriculture extend daily and it is difficult to see how even a compromise solution to this huge and widespread problem can be found. Man's needs must; and particularly where relatively primitive communities achieve increased survival and present larger food and power demands, the continued restriction of natural ecosystems threatens all but the most adaptable species. Thus while belated protective legislation on behalf of raptors fills more and more statute books, the living room of birds of prey still recedes and their sustenance may reduce. The issues that their conservers face are now international. We must wish their persuasions a full hearing and hope at least for some safe breeding, staging, and wintering grounds to be reserved for two marvellous orders of aerial beings.

It therefore needs to be repeated that no bird of prey is more than marginally or occasionally destructive to man's interests and that the great majority of raptors are either wholly beneficial or harmless, as they go about their ancestral business of, for example, predating granivorous rodents and reducing fly-blown carcasses to a few dry bones. This is not to write that they can turn back plagues of rats or hordes of locusts (both faster breeding organisms), but it is to show that given naturally abundant prey species, there is no

sign that more than the odd individual raptor has learned the new skills and habits required to sustain an attack on domestic or supported stocks of mammals and birds. It is now appreciated that the stable presence of successful predators in any ecosystem is the best evidence of its integrated health and hygiene. Thus the extermination of birds of prey loses man a highly significant indicator to his own security and recognition of such views has helped to turn the tide of harmful opinion and active persecution of raptors as supposedly criminal birds.

FIELD OBSERVATION OF RAPTORS

It would be wrong to conclude this introduction to the diurnal birds of prey without some comments on how to find and observe them. These must, however, be immediately prefaced by an appeal for a cautious approach to all but the commonest species at any time and for no disturbance to any during the breeding season.

The best method of finding raptors might be termed 'skyline-watching' since, except for those species that perch prominently, they are most easily spotted in the lower air spaces over open country and woodland. Thus when looking for raptors, observers should try to choose in their habitat those observation points that afford wide horizons and backgrounds above or against which the soaring or flying bird will present an obvious target. The horizons may be distant and broad, as over the taiga, or quite close and narrow, as across a reed marsh, but the visual activity of the observer will not vary from frequent scans (and considerable patience). Once a raptor is spotted by eye, it should be followed by the use of binoculars and tracked along its hunting route or its path to a nesting area. The former may be on a regular line and can be at least roughly mapped over several periods of observation. The latter may also be fixed but it should be noted that many raptors do not fly directly to their nests, purposely covering their final approach. Thus nest-finding takes far longer than the discovery of resident adults and is, in woodlands, a matter for exceptionally quiet and cautious searches on foot, with the eye preset to search canopies for entry points and old nests, and ground cover for tell-tale pellets, droppings, and moulted feathers. It is as well to begin nest searches downwind from the birds' last position and so minimize the chance of an approach being heard. On no account should this practice be reversed and the birds banged and beaten out of cover. With cliff-nesting species, nest-finding is a much simpler process. The birds frequently display over the breeding site and enter it directly, pitching at the nest. Once again, however, observers must hang back and do nothing to disturb normal behaviour. Disturbance of the nests of rarer species is illegal in many countries.

In winter, with most home ranges of raptors changed, 'skyline-watching' may produce results but quite rapid, automobile transects of open country offer an alternative (and warmer) method of observation. Like most birds, raptors appear not to connect a car with the human driver and many close views of them can be obtained through a carefully positioned car window. This also holds during the seasons of migrations and dispersal but in those, the classic method of raptor observation is the juxtaposition of birdwatcher and a narrow-front, overhead passage. The most famous of the European vantage points have already been mentioned in the notes on movements. Some part of their annual dramas can be enjoyed at many other, less obvious places, since almost any leading line of hills or coast and most islands can suddenly display migrant raptors. Their density is rarely so high that it merits constant scanning of the sky and observers should rather look out for the tell-tale panics of other birds, most obvious in sudden quiet or mass flushes. Whenever common landbirds and seagulls fly up suddenly and there is no obvious human or large animal predator in sight, the cause is usually the arrival of their fellow avian predator. Similarly, a hidden raptor may attract mobs of passerine birds, which draw courage from numbers and vent vociferously their displeasure at its presence. Among mobbing species, the most forward are often the larger thrushes and they may assist the observer's eye by flying at the hawk or falcon.

Really close views of raptors are generally hard to achieve, other than through carefully positioned hides. The best chances come with birds near their nests, in the terminal stage of hunting, or in possession of freshly killed prey. Once again observers must not press too close and so rob their subject of a chance to breed or feed.

The genera *Elanus* and *Milvus* occupy close systematic positions following *Pernis* and ahead of *Haliaeetus*. They are, however, very different in size, structure, behaviour, and flight action and character. The two *Milvus* species, the Red Kite and the Black Kite, are relatively large, long-winged, and long-tailed raptors. Their flight action is noticeably loose and free, with deep wing-beats alternated with effortless soaring and gliding on horizontal or slightly arched quills; when searching for food, their relatively small heads and loose tails hang down, the latter frequently also twisted. Their flight image is noticeably cruciform and at times 'hunch-backed'. Both the Red and Black Kite find hovering difficult but are adept at hanging on the wind, side-slips, wheels, and aerial snatches. Overlaps between their appearance and that of other raptors occur most with the Honey Buzzard, the Marsh Harrier, and the Booted Eagle. The *Elanus* species, the Black-winged Kite, is a relatively small, fairly long-winged but noticeably short-tailed bird of prey, with an owl-like head. Its flight action includes persistent skilful hovering (often with trailing feet), and alternation of flap and glide (with raised wings) when searching for food—both actions again recalling an owl or small harrier—and a faster flap when making speed—recalling a falcon. Its dive on to prey recalls that of the Kestrel, but is slower. The appearance of the Black-winged Kite is very distinctive when known. However, in a brief view it can suggest the other raptors just mentioned.

Of the structural differences shown by kites, the most trustworthy are the long, always clearly forked tail of the Red, and the 'unfingered' wing-point and the short, almost square tail of the Black-winged. The shallow tail-fork of the Black is not always visible (or present on worn or moulting birds) and it is this species that provokes most confusion with other raptors, particularly the female and young Marsh Harrier and the dark Booted Eagle.

In good light or at close range, the important plumage marks of kites are: the generally bright, boldly contrasting pattern of the Red Kite (**1–3**), with its almost white head, strongly orange underbody and upper tail, and noticeably pale or even white panels beneath most of the primaries and tail; the generally drab, less contrasting pattern of the Black (**4–7**), with its lack of warm tones, dull head, and underwing-panel in adult (**4** and **5**) and darker tail in both adult and immature (**6** and **7**); and the bold white, grey, and black pattern of the Black-winged (**8–10**), with its black shoulder patches creating a diagnostic character unique in West Palearctic raptors and the distinctly dappled saddle of the juvenile (**10**) allowing certain ageing. The greatest risks in kite identification lie in the relative brightness of wing-panels and ventral area of the juvenile Black (**6**), and the adult eastern Black (**7**). These frequently lead to mistaken claims of the Red Kite both within and outside its range.

Of the two *Milvus* kites, it is the Black that regularly forms flocks or loose streams on migration and uses rising air in the manner of other large, soaring raptors. The Red Kite is more often a solitary vagrant.

IW

2 **Red Kite** *Milvus milvus*
Black Kite *Milvus migrans*
Black-winged Kite *Elanus caeruleus*

The large-headed, short-tailed Black-winged Kite is restricted in the West Palearctic to Iberia, north-west Africa, and the Nile Valley, occurring in open, wooded lowlands. It feeds on small animals and nests (usually) in a tree. There are at least 60 pairs in Iberia but its numbers elsewhere are not known. Although normally sedentary, individuals have wandered north to The Netherlands and West Germany. The diagnostic black shoulders show on both adult (**6**) and juvenile (**7**).

The Black Kite is a uniformly coloured, often scruffy kite. Except in north-west Europe, it is one of the most widespread of West Palearctic raptors and inhabits steppe, open woodlands, and cultivation, especially in the vicinity of large waters. Highly adaptable, it is both a predator and a scavenger and has a wide diet including fish. It nests in a tree or on a ledge. Still a fairly common bird, there are up to 25 000 pairs in its Spanish stronghold and perhaps 50 000 pairs in the whole region. Primarily a long-distance migrant, it winters in Africa south of the Sahara. North-west orientated vagrancy has increased in recent years. Western birds always show black bills (adult, **2;** more scaly juvenile, **3**), the Egyptian birds have a yellow bill (**5**), and the eastern birds wear a darker head (**4**).

The Red Kite is a strongly patterned and richly coloured raptor, now restricted mainly to Iberia but also widely scattered in the rest of Europe south of 60°N and east to 45°E. Normally it nests in a tree and feeds on both live prey and carrion. Human persecution has reduced its numbers to about 12 500 pairs, which south of an axis from Wales south-east to Rumania are mainly primarily resident, but elsewhere withdraw in winter to Iberia and North Africa. The whitish head, scaled orange body and tail, and black primaries of the Red Kite (**1**) make a superb sight.

3 **White-tailed Eagle** *Haliaeetus albicilla*
Pallas's Fish Eagle *Haliaeetus leucoryphus*
African Fish Eagle *Haliaeetus vocifer*

The White-tailed Eagle is a huge, rather vulturine eagle. West of 25°E, it is now restricted mainly to coastal or riverain habitats; further east, it is more widespread around haunts of waterfowl or other food sources, which include carrion. It nests mainly on cliff-ledges. Greatly decreased, the total population of the West Palearctic does not much exceed 100 pairs. Most coastal birds are sedentary when adult but the eastern population is highly migratory, withdrawing south of 58–53°N. The juvenile (**2**) is shaggy and dark brown; the paler adult (**1**) is more immaculate, with hoary head and foreparts behind a huge yellow bill.

The African Fish Eagle has reached Sinai. The adult (**5**), is unmistakable; the juvenile (**6**) may be confused with the White-tailed Eagle until its black and white tail and white primary patches show.

The Pallas's Fish Eagle has straggled to Poland, Finland, and Norway. The adult (**3**), has a diagnostic black and white tail; the juvenile (**4**) might suggest several other eagles but such confusion will not persist when the bird flies (Plates 4 and 5).

The genus *Haliaeetus* occupies an early systematic position compared to the so-called true eagles *Aquila*, and their somewhat primitive generic character varies little in size, structure, and flight action. Such a form has more of a hint of that of the Old World vultures *Gyps*, particularly in the widely 'fingered' primaries and parallel-sides of fully outstretched wings. All three West Palearctic species are relatively large to huge, long-winged but rather short-tailed eagles. Their flight action is noticeably powerful, with more persistent shallow and measured wing-beats than in *Aquila* and more sporadic and shorter glides. The White-tailed Eagle has a noticeably slower flight action than the other two and both the African Fish Eagle and Pallas's Fish Eagle are relatively agile, with the ability to make aerial snatches. All soar with wings held level or arched slightly downwards; they lack any real hovering ability but may hang on the wind. Overlaps between their appearance and other eagles occur most with large *Aquila*, particulary the Spotted and the Imperial Eagle, but in brief glimpses the two smaller species may also suggest the Rough-legged Buzzard and the two *Milvus* kites.

In good light or at close range, some plumage marks of the fish eagles can be very obvious but it must be stressed that they vary according to age. The White-tailed Eagle (**1** and **2**) is overall the darkest and drabbest, with its under-pattern showing little relief (except for indistinct streaks on chest and tail feathers) in the immature (**2**) but with a pale grey-white head and often noticeably short, white tail in the adult (**1**). The under patterns of the African Fish Eagle (**3** and **4**) and the Pallas's Fish Eagle (**5** and **6**) present several pitfalls, notably the overlap in tail pattern (compare **4** and **5**). In juveniles, the pure white panels on the primaries and across the chest of the African Fish Eagle (**4**) are more boldly contrasting than the dull marks of the Pallas's Fish Eagle (**6**) which are, however, dangerously reminiscent of several immature *Aquila* eagles (see Plate 27). In adults, the white head and chest, dark but bright rufous underbody, and pure white vent and tail of the African Fish Eagle (**3**) are very obvious. The first two of these characters are partly shown by the Pallas's Fish Eagle (**5**) but its tail is boldly banded black at the tip, like that of the juvenile of the African Fish Eagle (**4**) and unlike that of its own young which resembles that of the White-tailed Eagle (compare **6** with **2**).

Adulthood and final plumages are not achieved by the *Haliaeetus* eagles for at least five years (eight in the case of the White-tailed) and all their plumages are subject to irregular moult and wear. It is important, therefore, to consider the possible variations between the plumages shown opposite (and in Plate 5). It should also be remembered that the *Aquila* eagles show similarly protracted plumage progressions though none but the Tawny Eagle becomes as dishevelled as young *Haliaeetus* eagles, whose tails suffer from the rather vertical perching attitude of the genus and can become as short as those of vultures.

1

2

3

4

5

6

IW

5 Fish eagles in flight from above

The variations in the upperpart patterns of the fish eagles mirror those of their undersides. In juvenile plumage, the White-tailed Eagle (2) is noticeably dark and uniform in appearance, the African Fish Eagle (4) shows the most relief in plumage marks—with its white-flecked greater wing-coverts and rump and white tail-base very obvious—and the Pallas's Fish Eagle (6) exhibits the most confusing pattern—with grey tips to greater wing-coverts and uppertail-coverts yielding marks recalling those of similarly aged Spotted and sub-adult Imperial and Steppe Eagles. In adult plumage, the white head, rather grey back and wing-coverts, and white tail of the White-tailed Eagle (1) produce a markedly different appearance from that of its juvenile, but even so this lacks the basic black and white contrast of the other two species. Between the adults of the African Fish Eagle (3) and the Pallas's Fish Eagle (5), the most striking plumage differences are the pure white head, rump, and tail of the former and the tawny upper mantle, black rump, and black basal and distal bands on the white tail of the latter.

The vulturine character and appearance of the Haliaeetus eagles is well shown here. When extended, their wings lack the quite marked variations in outline shown by those of the Aquila eagles and only the Pallas's Fish Eagle (5 and 6) has a tail that approaches the proportional length of any other eagle. The projection of the relatively long bills and heads should also be noted; it is a constant character in the Haliaeetus eagles, being most obvious in the White-tailed.

Once again, the slow and often erratic plumage progression can create confusion between these large raptors. Although their occurrence in the same area is extremely unlikely, the appearance of sub-adult African and Pallas's Fish Eagles in their second year could well be very similar. Their tail pattern is also not dissimilar to that of the young Golden Eagle (Plate 28). Such overlaps in a striking feature afford examples of the very real traps of large raptor identifications. They must be guarded against at all times, even by expert observers.

Although occasionaly seen in loose parties, most observations of sedentary or migrant birds will be of solitary individuals.

6 Lammergeier *Gypaetus barbatus*
Egyptian Vulture *Neophron percnopterus*
Hooded Vulture *Necrosyrtes monachus*

The Hooded Vulture has wandered to Mauritania and Morocco. Thin-billed, small-headed, and pink-faced, this vulture shows a grey hood in the adult (**6**) and a brown one in the juvenile (**7**).

The Lammergeier is a relatively slim but still large vulturine raptor, possessing a remarkable habit of bone-breaking (by repeated dropping from a height). Its falcon-like form is marked at all times. In the West Palearctic, it is now largely restricted to high mountain ranges in the south. There are 30 or so pairs in the Pyrénées, another 30–40 pairs in Greece, and up to 500 pairs in Turkey, with few elsewhere. They nest in large fissures or on sheltered ledges and are mainly sedentary. The adult (**1**) is among the most colourful of all large raptors. The juvenile (**2**) is dull by comparison, with even the adult pattern broken by its dark neck and upper breast.

The Egyptian Vulture is a long-billed, full-necked, but relatively lightly-built vulture, widely scattered in the West Palearctic, with a population of about 3500 pairs densest in north-west Africa, Iberia, Greece, and Turkey. The Egyptian Vulture nests on a ledge or in a fissure. North of 28°N the bird is a summer visitor, withdrawing to south of the Sahara in winter. Vagrants have reached north-west Europe. The pale adult (**3**) with its orange face differs markedly from the juvenile (**5**) which is almost all brown except for a pale lower back. Sub-adults (**4**) are increasingly adult-like.

7 Black Vulture *Aegypius monachus*
Lappet-faced Vulture *Torgos tracheliotos*
Griffon Vulture *Gyps fulvus*
Rüppell's Vulture *Gyps rueppellii*

A vagrant to Egypt, the Rüppell's Vulture is similar in size and structure to the Griffon Vulture. The adult (**7**) is distinguished by the beautiful scaling of its upperparts and the immature (**8**) by its darker head and neck.

The Lappet-faced Vulture, second only in size to the Black Vulture, outclasses all its relatives in power and majesty. There is a handful of pairs nesting in Israel. The pink, loose-skinned head and neck are brighter in the adult (**3**) than in the juvenile (**4**). The white thighs (and body down) of the adult also catch the eye.

The unpatterned Black Vulture has the deepest bill and greatest bulk of all vultures. In the West Palearctic it is now restricted to montane wildernesses to the south of 45°N, where under 900 pairs nest in trees. Although primarily a resident, the odd sub-adult may roam widely in Europe. Its black-brown plumage contrasts with a pale head and bill, almost white in the adult (**1**) and buffy-pink in the juvenile (**2**), and yellow to pale grey feet.

The Griffon Vulture is a long-necked, huge vulture, lacking the complete majesty of the last two species. In the West Palearctic it has held its ground better than the Black Vulture and still occurs widely in and around the Mediterranean. About 6000 pairs remain, mostly in Spain, and nest in fissures and on ledges. Unlike the Black Vulture, the Griffon Vulture is a partially migratory species. Its plumage pattern shows much relief compared to the other large vultures, but the differences between adult (**5**) and juvenile (**6**) are not marked other than in the warmer tone of the latter.

The single-species *Gypaetus, Neophron*, and *Necrosyrtes* precede systematically their bulkier relatives, and the fully adult birds present noticeably individual form and appearances in flight which are not always evident in sub-adults and juveniles. At these younger ages, size, structural characters, and slight pattern marks are important to diagnosis. Of the three species, two—the Lammergeier and the Egyptian Vulture—lack the relative breadth of wing so typical of most vultures and have diamond-shaped tails. The former is, however, a much larger bird (with its wingspan 50 per cent wider) and has the narrowest and most pointed outer wing of any vulture, which promotes, along with the long tail, a markedly falcon-like appearance. The Hooded Vulture is much bulkier than the Egyptian, with proportionately the broadest wings of any vulture in the West Palearctic and an insignificant, wedge-shaped tail. When its size is not evident, it frequently suggests other species of vultures of the genera *Aegypius* and *Torgos* (Plate 10).

The flight actions of the three also vary. Thus though all may soar on wings stretched out and level, the Lammergeier has a characteristically deep and powerful wing-beat when initiating a glide on slightly bowed wings, the Egyptian Vulture shows a marked incidence of active flaps and has the unusual habit, after a series of flaps, of holding its wings momentarily flat before adopting a bowed gliding position, while the Hooded Vulture combines quite fast wing-beats with the outstretched and angled wing positions of its bulkier relatives (in *Gyps, Torgos,* and

Aegypius). The Lammergeier frequently patrols close to the land surface, a habit that increases its resemblance to a huge falcon.

In good light or at close range, the predominantly white head and white to orange nape and underbody of the adult Lammergeier (**1** and **2**) contrast markedly with its otherwise mainly black plumage, which shows much sheen on the larger feathers at certain light angles. The immature Lammergeier (**3**) is much duller, with brown-black the dominant plumage tone, and its dark head and breast-hood contrasting with the dull pale brown or ochre underbody. At all ages, tail length in this species is emphasized from below by the contrast of pale vent and dark tail. Plumage progression in the Egyptian Vulture is complex, beginning with the almost uniform juvenile (**7**), passing through four increasingly pied immatures (**6** the first) and ending with the vividly contrasting adult (**4** and **5**), which is unmistakable when well seen. At a great height it may be, however, confused with other soaring birds such as the light morph of the Booted Eagle, the White Stork, and even the White Pelican. Confusion between the young Egyptian Vulture and Lammergeier is also possible, but the former's pale throat, increasingly pale wing-lining, and never black tail—combined with much smaller size—should prevent this in most views. Compared to the other two, the plumage pattern of the Hooded Vulture (**8** and **9**) is consistently more uniform. Its dark wing-lining, contrasting with the pale marks over the bases of all quills, and its noticeably pale head and feet are all constant features.

9 Old World vultures in flight (2)

The two *Gyps* species are classic representatives of the group of carrion-eating vultures and occupy a central systematic position within it. Both are small-headed, short-tailed but long- and broad-winged, huge raptors; their primaries are markedly 'fingered' in flight but their long necks show only during take-off and landing attitudes. Both the Griffon Vulture and Rüppell's Vulture share a similar flight action, with slow, deep wing-beats rarely used except during take-off and progressive flight achieved by soaring and then gliding. During the latter stage their wings may be flexed, this flexing becoming acute in descents to roosts or carrion. The only marked difference in specific flight action is in the wing position for soaring and slow gliding, with that of the Griffon Vulture distinctly raised above the horizontal and that of Rüppell's Vulture markedly level. Their sturdy legs trail noticeably just before landing.

In good light or at close range, both the Griffon and Rüppell's Vultures exhibit distinctive plumage patterns, with the former (1–3) always showing a fairly bold contrast between its ochre-buff body and wing-coverts and its black quills, and the latter (4–6) showing a generally darker, less contrasting, but more marked appearance, with the sharp scalloped edges of most wing-coverts and back feathers in the adult (4 and 5) instantly diagnostic. The juvenile Rüppell's Vulture (6) is less distinctive but, from below, lacks the marked contrast between the wing-lining and quills so typical of the Griffon Vulture at all ages. Rüppell's Vulture is always darker headed than the Griffon Vulture.

Wild vultures are only exceptional vagrants to north-west and northern parts of the West Palearctic but captive birds of various species, including the Turkey Vulture of North America (only distantly related), do occasionally escape, first exciting and then disappointing their observers. Confusion between the *Gyps* vultures and the large eagles is possible at long range, but the former are truly huge. They also maintain the most persistant 'fixed wing' attitudes and have the most fanned and 'fingered' primaries. Their flight is generally much less agile in enclosed air-spaces and unlike eagles, they never utter far-carrying calls. Their behaviour also differs, with social systems in carrion-searching and cliff-roosting well developed and the former leading to the classic gatherings at dead animals. At these, there is a distinct 'peck-order' among the vultures. Set in the main by size and power; it is led by the Lappet-faced and Black Vultures and ends with the Egyptian Vulture and the other part-time carrion eaters such as the Tawny Eagle and the Black Kite.

The Griffon Vulture often patrols and circles in small groups but the Black Vulture (Plate 10) usually remains solitary in the sky, until there is a general descent to newfound carrion.

The monotypic genera *Torgos* and *Aegypius* complete the systematic span of vultures in the West Palearctic and probably represent the evolutionary culmination of that group. Both are larger than any other member and the Black Vulture is an immense raptor on the wing. Both it and the Lappet-faced Vulture exhibit tremendous power and in appearance they are the most impressive of all vultures. Their flight action is similar to that of *Gyps* but is even more accomplished, with regular, deep wing-beats on take-off (and occasionally during flight) and effortless soaring and gliding along cliffs and in the sky. During the latter actions, both adopt level wing positions with just a hint of bowing beyond the carpal joint during more flexed, gliding attitudes. These positions are thus distinct from the raised wings of a soaring Griffon Vulture. The 'fingering' of primaries is marked in both the Lappet-faced and Black Vultures, that of the latter being the most separated of any vulture except during flexed wing attitudes when the quills become noticeably bunched. The relatively shorter, thicker neck and massive head of the Black Vulture is sometimes discernible.

At longer ranges, both Lappet-faced and Black are essentially uniformly black vultures and show no obvious relief in their plumage pattern. In good light or at close range the adult Black Vulture (**1–3**) shows its obviously pale head and feet well, and its slightly paler inner quill webs and paler greater coverts can show against the black wing-lining and 'fingers'. Only the juvenile Black Vulture (**2**) is truly black, lacking the brown tone of its parents and not showing the paler shade across the under greater coverts and over the base of the undertail. It differs little from the juvenile Lappet-faced Vulture (**6**) which is browner and shows a smaller, paler head, duller feet, and a shorter tail. The adult Lappet-faced Vulture (**4** and **5**) is less intensely black above than the Black Vulture and its wing-linings and underbody are boldly marked with buff and white in a characteristic 'skeletal' pattern. The pink folds of skin (lappets) can be surprisingly visible in close flight. The tail of the Black Vulture, when unworn, is more wedge-shaped than those of the Lappet-faced Vulture, Rüppell's Vulture, and the Griffon Vulture.

At a distance, confusion is possible between these vultures and the uniformly dark eagles, such as adult Spotted and immature White-tailed. The latter generally exhibit more protruding and darker heads, longer and usually square tails and different proportions between their tails and their rarely as straight-sided wings. The best chances of separation lie in structure and silhouette. Because of their relative scarcity, it is very unusual to see the Black and Lappet-faced Vultures in more than singles or very small groups.

3

2

1

5

4

6

IW

The genera *Circaetus* and *Terathopius* are essentially African in origin, and are systematically and behaviourally distinct form the other eagles. In many circumstances, *Circaetus* is reminiscent of a large *Buteo* buzzard but *Terathopius* has a form unique in the world, let alone the West Palearctic, with a ridiculously short tail and a laterally swinging flight action. It is quite the strangest raptor of the region covered by this book.

In more precise terms, the Short-toed Eagle is a medium-sized, broad-faced, long-tailed snake-eagle, with its long wings also showing remarkable breadth behind the carpal area when flexed. Its flight action combines shades of *Buteo* (in the slightly forward position of flat or slightly raised wings when soaring), the smaller *Aquila* eagles (in the slightly drooped primary set and forward-extended carpal joint when gliding), and even kites *Milvus* (in the tilting of its sharp-cornered, square tail). Its wing-beats are strong, recalling the powerful strokes of large eagles, and can be fast, allowing the bird to hover. In contrast to the proportions of the Short-toed Eagle, the aerial form of the Bateleur is quite extraordinary with its large, ruffed head and long, basally bulging, then distally tapering wings dwarfing its body and very short tail. In the adult, the tail does not extend past the relaxed feet and the body shape ends abruptly. The flight action of the Bateleur is correspondingly strange, with a burst of fast, flat wing-beats on take-off accelerating it into markedly sustained sailing, accompanied by frequent lateral shifts and swings. When sailing, soaring, and gliding, the wings are raised in a distinct V. It is doubted whether the Bateleur's configuration can sustain low-speed flight; yet the bird is capable of high speed rolls and stoops and the noise of its wing-beats is loud and far-carrying.

The two snake-eagles are quite distinct in plumage pattern and colours. The Short-toed Eagle (**1–4**) recalls a pale buzzard and, as in that group, its plumage variations are marked, particularly below, where on a white ground every gradation between dark-hooded and heavily-barred birds (**1**) to pale-headed, buff-chested, and only finely marked ones (**2**) occurs. All lack, however, the dark carpal patches of the Honey Buzzard and Buzzard (Plate 20), some *Hieraaetus* eagles, and Osprey (Plate 29), and the tail always shows three obvious bands. The upperparts of the Short-toed Eagle vary much less (**3** and **4**). It cannot be aged in flight but the Bateleur can be, since the juvenile (**7**) is quite unlike its parents (male **6** and **9**, female **5** and **8**), with a brown-black plumage relieved only by a buff head and pale-based quills. The apparent dimorphism of the adult Bateleur which sports both chestnut-backed and cream-mantled birds is unproved but the sexual differences are well established, with the female from above (**8**) showing an additional pale wing-panel across the inner quills which are uniformly black in the male (**9**). From below, the fully black inner quills of the male show again (compare **6** with **5**).

On days of heavy passage, the Short-toed Eagle may form groups or loose streams along a flight path. In other circumstances, most views are of single birds.

12 Short-toed Eagle *Circaetus gallicus*
Bateleur *Terathopius ecaudatus*

The Short-toed Eagle is a broad-faced, usually dark-hooded eagle, representing the African snake-eagles in the West Palearctic. A bird of southern latitudes in the west, it reaches 60°N in Russia and inhabits open ground or valleys, nesting in low trees. Over 5000 pairs still nest in Europe (3000 pairs in Spain), and all withdraw to winter in the northern tropics of Africa. Its buzzard-like appearance is obvious at close range, with distinctions between adult and juvenile sunk in a range of light to dark morphs. Most birds show bold marks on the underbody (2) and a tri-banded tail (1). The long tarsi are a striking character.

A vagrant to Iraq, the Bateleur is an almost mythological, aberrant snake-eagle, with the most colourful pattern of any Old World raptor. The hen (4) but not the cock (3) shows a white panel on the secondaries. The juvenile (5) is undistinguished.

13 Marsh Harrier *Circus aeruginosus*
Hen Harrier *Circus cyaneus*
Montagu's Harrier *Circus pygargus*
Pallid Harrier *Circus macrourus*

When perched, all the harriers show relatively small and broad heads, long bodies and tails, full thighs, and long slender legs. Their plumage patterns divide into the grey and white of the adult male Hen, Montagu's, and Pallid and the mainly brown and variably marked of the adult male Marsh and all females and immatures. All nest on the ground.

The Marsh Harrier is the most widely distributed species, inhabiting aquatic habitats from 30° to 67°N, and maintaining a total population in Europe of perhaps some 9000 pairs. North-eastern birds withdraw south of the Sahara. The dark brown adult female (2) and typical juvenile (3) have a markedly cream head. The adult cock (1) shows a white head and mainly grey secondaries and tail.

The Hen Harrier is the most northerly species, reaching 70°N in Fenno-Scandia. It migrates throughout Europe, becoming concentrated in the west and south in winter. At least 5000 pairs survive in Europe in dry, open habitats. The adult male (4) has a full hood and unmarked inner wings. The adult hen (5) and immature are predominantly brown, with ruffed heads and streaked underparts.

The range of the Montagu's Harrier shadows that of the Marsh Harrier, though it is more local in central and south-east Europe even though it can use the niches of both the Marsh and Hen Harriers. Its much reduced European population of about 8000 pairs winters south of the Sahara. The adult male (6) is dingier than the Hen and Pallid Harriers, with a black bar visible on the folded wing and rufous streaks on the underbody; the adult female (7) is smaller than the Hen, with a dark cheek emphasizing the white rear surround to the eye. The juvenile has an unstreaked rufous underbody.

The Pallid Harrier rarely occurs west of 28°E and withdraws south to the east Mediterranean and the African savannas in winter. The adult male (9) is very pale, being completely white below; the adult female (10) and the juvenile have a distinct white surround to their dark cheeks. Some juveniles are as pale as honey below.

The genus *Circus* has four West Palearctic members. All share a common flight silhouette of relatively small but broad head, long body and tail, long wings, and—in some attitudes—dangling legs. They also show a common and equally distinctive flight action which includes both loose active flapping and long, low-level and wandering erratic glides with wings held up in a V. Their hunting behaviour includes obvious hovering above and quartering over prey habitats. The field identification of the Marsh Harrier is relatively simple. Separation of the other species is often difficult, with many flight observations at long range being inconclusive, while the overlaps of plumage patterns are still incompletely researched.

Unlike its three congeners, the Marsh Harrier (**1–5**) has a predominatly dark plumage and the female and immature may be virtually uniform in colour (**3**) or, more usually, show a striking yellow-cream head and similarly coloured leading edges to the inner wing (**2** and **4**). All females and immatures may suggest Black Kites and a good view of their heads, underwing pattern, and tail shape is essential to distant diagnosis. The adult male Marsh Harrier (**1** and **5**), is boldly patterned above and below. Its rufous wing-linings, chocolate back, and upper wing-coverts and dark vent are diagnostic in combination. Unlike its three congeners, the Hen Harrier (**6–9**) sports a large white rump in all plumages. This mark is responsible for the term 'ring-tail' loosely applied to the females and immatures of the Hen (**7** and **9**), Montagu's, and Pallid

Harriers (Plate 15). Such overlaps in appearance between the Hen Harrier and the two smaller *Circus* species are many. Separation of males is not too difficult; the all or mostly black outer primaries, the dark trailing edge along the other quills, and the grey hood of the male Hen Harrier (**6** and **8**) are diagnostic in combination. Distinguishing females is not easy; the large size, broad wings, indistinctly marked head, and heavily streaked underbody of the female Hen Harrier (**7** and **9**) are diagnostic in combination. Defining the specific identity of immatures may be impossible, though once again the large size and stronger body streaks and wing barring of the Hen Harrier form the most obvious clues of any young 'ring-tail'. Rumours of juvenile Hen Harriers with unstreaked rufous-ochre underbodies have never been confirmed in print but they have prevented any certain European record of the Nearctic form of the species, the so-called Marsh Hawk.

The Marsh and Hen Harriers are, respectively, the largest and second largest of the *Circus* quartet, with noticeably broader wings and heavier build than the Montagu's and Pallid Harriers. Both Marsh and Hen Harriers also show five obvious 'fingers' at their wing-tips; Montagu's and Pallid show four.

On passage, all the harriers appear to move on a broad front, with occasional concentrations showing in thin streams and rare groupings. When indulging in rare soaring, a Marsh Harrier among Black Kites sets a real challenge even to expert observers.

The two smallest *Circus* species, the Montagu's and Pallid Harriers, are close to the Hen Harrier in plumage colours and pattern, and approach each other in such characters even more so. Compared to the Hen Harrier, they are both smaller, slighter, and noticeably narrower-winged. These differences in size and structure are directly reflected in their flight action, which in any mode is lighter and even more buoyant. They are truly graceful raptors with an obvious mastery of lower airspace. In both the Montagu's and Pallid Harriers, plumage progression is complex in the male and there is an added complication in the former's occasional partial or total melanism which causes dark morphs to occur in both juvenile and later plumages at any age, particularly in the male (**9**). In normally coloured males, the Pallid Harrier (**1** and **4**) fully merits its name and its pale grey upperparts and white body immediately recall those of an adult gull. This illusion is heightened by the very restricted area of black on the five longest primaries which creates only a black notch in, rather than a solid patch across, the wing-tip. The male Montagu's Harrier (**6** and **10**) is noticeably darker than the Pallid or Hen, with its sullied grey tone, the largest black area on the primaries of all harriers, and various other plumage reliefs, most noticeable in the transverse black bars across the secondaries (two visible from below, one from above) and the grey bars on the outer tail-feathers. The streaking of wing-lining and lower body adds to its relatively dingy appearance.

In the case of the females and immatures, the separation of the Montagu's and Pallid Harriers becomes difficult, even impossible. The best opportunities come with juveniles, for the Montagu's Harrier (**8**) is typically deep rufous on the wing-lining and underbody while the Pallid Harrier (**3**) is paler there, often markedly so. The best distinguishing character is difficult to see in flight, though it does sometimes catch the eye in overhead and side views. It is the distinct pale collar around the dark cheeks of the Pallid Harrier, also shown by females (**2**). Apart from this mark, the female Montagu's Harrier (**7**) is very similar to the Pallid (**2**) but her separation is, in a well lit, close view, supported by the lack of a grey tinge to her upperparts and the stronger barring which is visible on both surfaces of her secondaries. It is important to remember that both the Montagu's and Pallid Harriers are distinctly smaller and more slightly built than the Hen Harrier. With experience, their lightness can be quickly spotted and concentration then quickly directed to the fine points that allow their separation.

During daylight, whether hunting or migrating, the small harriers typically move with wide spaces between individuals. These are maintained in their African winter quarters and break down only at dusk, when small roosting groups gather together.

16 Dark Chanting Goshawk *Melierax metabates*
Goshawk *Accipiter gentilis*

The Dark Chanting Goshawk, the single West Palearctic representative of a central and south African genus of savanna-haunting hawks, is restricted to central Morocco. It nests deep in a thorn-tree. The adult (**5**) is a greyish hawk, with strikingly marked tail and bright red cere and legs. The immature (**6**) recalls the Honey Buzzard and other hawks, but the combination of its dark chest and fully barred underparts and rump are diagnostic.

The strong-billed, mean-eyed, long-headed, relatively huge Goshawk shows a strongly etched supercilium and dark cheeks in all plumages. The most powerful *Accipiter*, the hen can be up to a fifth larger than the cock. It is essentially a woodland raptor, widely distributed in the West Palearctic from 35° to 70°N. A south-west shift occurs in its northern communities. Although ruthlessly persecuted by gamekeepers, its total European population still stands at over 18 000 pairs, which nest in trees. The adult male (**1** and **4**) has a dark grey or blue-grey back and is finely barred black on its white (never rufous-toned) underbody. The adult female (**2**) is dusky-brown above and prominently barred below. The juvenile (**3**) is more intricately patterned, with the characteristic streaks and spots of its underbody always obvious and allowing certain ageing.

17 Sparrowhawk *Accipiter nisus*
Levant Sparrowhawk *Accipiter brevipes*
Shikra *Accipiter badius*

When perched, the medium-sized to small hawks present markedly similar form—with relatively small bills, rounded heads, rather broad-chested bodies, obvious tails, and long thighs and legs—and like adult plumage patterns—with barred underparts, fully washed or shaded rufous in males. The identification of immatures is difficult. All nest in trees or bushes.

The Sparrowhawk occupies much the same range as the Goshawk, but its wider habitat tolerance allows it to inhabit farmland. Thus its population is much larger, with at least 80 000 pairs in the West Palearctic from which the northern communities withdraw in winter. The second largest *Accipiter* is therefore the most familiar member of its tribe and a key species in hawk identification. The adult male (**1**) is intensely coloured, blue-grey above and rufous below, even on the face. The noticeably larger adult female (**2**) and the immature (**3**) are essentially dark brown above, fully barred below. Their supercilia are less obvious than those of the Goshawk, even at close range.

The Levant Sparrowhawk is restricted to the south-east of the region, inhabiting mainly wooded river basins and plains. It is everywhere scarce, its population being numbered in only hundreds of pairs, and virtually disappears in winter, passing down the Nile Valley to unknown areas in Africa. Sexual differences in size and appearance are little marked but the adult cock (**4**) is bluer above and more rufous-pink below than the hen (**5**). The juvenile (**6**) differs from the Sparrowhawk in its spotted underbody.

The Shikra (male **7**, female **8**, juvenile **9**) occasionally breeds in eastern Russia. It is the smallest *Accipiter*, resembling the Levant Sparrowhawk but with even soft plumage tones and weaker barring or spotting on the underparts. A dark line down the throat is evident in all plumages but this mark is also shown by the young Levant Sparrowhawk.

18 Broad-winged hawks in flight from above

The broad-winged hawks *Melierax* and *Accipiter* occupy a systematic position between *Circus* and *Buteo*. All possess the ability to catch flying prey in close-quarter flight at, or just above, the land surface (often in cover) and the structural characters and actions that allow this. These are broad flexible wings, rapid wing-beats, long and full tails, sudden manoeuvres, and long legs for easy gripping. *Melierax* shows little sexual size difference, but in *Accipiter* specific size is subject to wide sexual overlaps through all four West Palearctic species. The field identifications of individual birds are therefore subject to unusual pitfalls. In more precise terms, the most telling structural characters in the group are the uniformly broad and parallel-sided wings and long rounded tail of the Dark Chanting Goshawk (**1** and **2**), the large head, deep chest, bulging secondaries, and long tail of the Goshawk (**3** and **4**), the rather broad but not deep chest, fairly broad and rounded wings, and usually square-ended tail of the Sparrowhawk (**5–7**), the narrower wings and generally rather falcon-like silhouette of the Levant Sparrowhawk (**11–13**), and the relatively small wing and tail size but compact build of the Shikra (**8 –10**).

Confusing overlaps recur in the patterns of their upperparts. Only the Dark Chanting Goshawk with its harrier-like plumage is distinctive in all plumages, the white area on the upperwing of the adult (**1**) appearing to 'flash' with each shallow beat and the pale rump and black-barred tail obvious from behind at any age (**1** and **2**). Among *Accipiter*, the most telling marks in their upperparts are the dark grey to brown tone and distinct supercilium of the Goshawk (**3** and **4**), the dark blue-grey tone and the black-barred tail of the male Sparrowhawk (**5**), the black wing-tips and pale blue-grey tone of the male Levant Sparrowhawk (**11**), and the very pale blue-grey tone of the male Shikra (**8**). The upperpart distinctions in the females and immatures are much less marked and the best chances for diagnosis are all found in the markings on their underparts. The greyer upperparts of the adult females of the Levant Sparrowhawk (**12**) and Shikra (**9**) frequently serve to invite confusion with the males of other species.

It is important to recognize the huge size range shown by these hawks in flight. The female Goshawk (**4**) is as large as a small buzzard (but has a much longer tail). The Dark Chanting Goshawk (**1** and **2**) matches the small harriers (but lacks their slim, often angled wings). The other species all overlap in size with the falcons, with the Shikra (**8–10**) being almost as small as the Merlin. Where their behaviour or their flight action also recalls other small raptors, the chances of mistaken identification are high.

Among these hawks, only the Levant Sparrowhawk migrates in flocks and marked streams which may contain hundreds of birds. The others appear singly or in small parties overnight.

Underviews of broad-winged hawks allow easier perception of certain structural characters, for example the even planes of the wings of the Dark Chanting Goshawk, the buzzard-like bulk—and particularly the broad, deep chest—of the female Goshawk, the slimness (relative to the Sparrowhawk) of the Levant Sparrowhawk, and the small bunched form of the Shikra.

As with the upper plumage patterns (Plate 18), the under plumage patterns of these hawks range from the distinctive—as in the male Hen Harrier-like image of the male Dark Chanting Goshawk (1) to the indistinctive—as in the male Goshawk (4) and female Sparrowhawk (9), and it is important for any observer (beginner or expert) to be able to recall quickly the truly diagnostic marks. They are given below.

Adults

Chanting Goshawk (1): grey hood extending to chest; black outer primaries; white or grey elsewhere, with broad-banded tail; red legs.

Goshawk: female (3) much larger than male (4); extensively barred below, but with contrasting and hence noticeably conspicuous white vent (especially in female); broad, dark-banded tail.

Sparrowhawk: female (9) much larger than male (10); female quite heavily barred below, hence often showing pale vent, male similarly marked but with rufous (not black-brown) and hence less obviously barred; noticeably dark-banded tail.

Levant Sparrowhawk: female (7) slightly larger than male (6), both showing noticeably black tips to primaries, forming striking black end to pale underwing and heightening falcon-like image, and pale narrowly dark-banded tail (with five fully visible bars, not four as in Sparrowhawk); males may be very pale, females may show as much colour on underbody as male Sparrowhawk.

Shikra: female (13) larger than male (12); both showing pattern closer to Levant Sparrowhawk than to Sparrowhawk, but lacking any obvious barring even on tail.

Juveniles

Dark Chanting Goshawk (1): brown chest; pale brown barring on body and wing-lining; grey-shaded and -barred secondaries; all features again recalling 'ring-tail' *Circus*.

Goshawk (5): heavily streaked, not barred, on wing-lining and body; ground of both buff (not rufous); primary-tips and tail-bands darker than in adult.

Sparrowhawk: male (11) raggedly barred, not streaked, on body; colour of female identical to adult male, of male less rufous than adult female; tail pattern as adult.

Levant Sparrowhawk (8): heavily lined with bold spots on body, barred on wing-lining; tail pattern as adult; throat streak unlikely to show in flight.

Shikra (14): pattern much as Levant Sparrowhawk but all feather marks noticeably paler, especially on wing-lining.

The genus *Pernis* is considered to be more primitive than *Buteo*, and contains in the West Palearctic only one member, the Honey Buzzard. It is, however, closely similar in appearance to the true buzzards. As in the widespread Buzzard, of which two races occur in the region, its plumage is extremely variable, and thus the separation of these two species and the other two *Buteo* is difficult, with structural characters, wing positions, and flight-actions crucial to accurate diagnosis. All these birds are rather large, long- and fairly broad-winged, full-tailed raptors; their flight actions contain both active flapping and passive soaring and sailing, with wing positions and outlines varied between these modes. They share with eagles a common classic silhouette of relatively small head (when fully extended), straight outstretched wings, bulky body, and (when expanded) broadly fanned tail, but show only five (not usually six) 'fingered' primaries and small beaks.

Looked at closely, the multiple images of buzzards do show some differences. Between the Honey Buzzard and the Buzzard, these are most obvious in the often upward extension of small head and slender neck, the broader mid-wing area, and the long, often closely-folded tail of the former and in the broad head, the short neck, and the relatively shorter, sharp-cornered tail of the latter. There is an even more distinct dichotomy in soaring and gliding attitudes, with wings held well raised or flat in the Buzzard and flat or drooping (along the outer half) in the Honey Buzzard. The latter often twists its tail noticeably and can then resemble the *Milvus* kites, while both may be taken for the Booted Eagle or the Short-toed Eagle.

Even in good light or at close range, there are few helpful plumage marks on the upperparts of buzzards. The Honey Buzzard (**1**) may show, however, a pale head, a grey cast over the whole wing-span and tail, and (on most) dark bands on the wings' trailing edges and across the base and end of the tail. The Buzzard never shows the last, its tail being narrowly barred grey in the Common (**5**) and rufous in the Steppe (**9**).

There are many patterns to be seen on the variable underparts of buzzards, of which all show black 'fingers' and carpal patches and most also a terminal tail-band. Otherwise the variability between species and age can only be learnt with long experience. Patterns diagnostic of the Honey Buzzard are the heavy chevrons and bars of intermediate and paler morphs (**2** and **4**), the heavy quill-bars of dark morphs (**3**), and the constant, irregularly spaced position (in adults) of two basal and one distal tail-bands. Sadly the juvenile lacks the last mark, but it still shows stronger quill-bars than in the Buzzard. No patterns diagnostic of the Buzzard exist, though the dark chest of most pale and intermediate birds (**6** and **7**) and the soft barring on the quills (also **8**) are usually helpful in any distinction from the Honey Buzzard. It is very important to recognize the close similarity of the Steppe Buzzard (**10** and **11**) to the Long-legged Buzzard (Plate 21) and to take particular care with really dark birds (**8**).

IW

Among the three *Buteo* species in the West Palearctic, size increases from the Buzzard through the Rough-legged Buzzard to the Long-legged Buzzard. With larger bulk and longer wings and tail comes a more aquiline and less compact appearance. Thus the general character of the Rough-legged and Long-legged Buzzards is often distinct from that of the Buzzard, most notably in slower and more elastic wing-beats, rather more attenuated and looser flight silhouettes, and less noticeably raised wings in soaring attitudes. Such differences can recall particularly the Golden Eagle and, in distant views, initial confusion between these birds and that eagle can occur. It should be noted that obvious structural differences between the two larger buzzards have yet to be perceived and may well be non-existent.

Happily the plumages of the Rough-legged and the Long-legged Buzzards are not difficult to tell apart, even when the latter is in atypical dress. The best marks are undoubtedly the tail patterns, essentially white with a broad dark terminal band in the Rough-legged Buzzard (**7** and **8**)— with narrower subterminal bands rarely obvious (**9**)— and strongly pink or pinkish-white in the Long-legged Buzzard (**1** and **2**), with normally no transverse marks visible on adults, with three to four narrow bands on typical immatures (**3** and **4**) and complete barring on the uncommon dark morph (**6**). After the tail patterns, the most useful characters are the Red Kite-like tri-colours of the typical adult Long-legged Buzzard (**1** and **2**), with orange-brown wing-coverts and central body set off by the mainly white undersurface of quills and the black carpal patches, vent, and wing-rim; and the two-tone, brown-black, and white colours of the Rough-legged Buzzard (**7–9**), with its black carpal patches, wing-rim, (variably sized) thigh patches, and rump constant in all birds.

Unfortunately there are dangerous overlaps in appearance between the Long-legged Buzzard and the other buzzards. Particular pitfalls are set by immature (**4**) and dark adult (**5** and **6**) Long-legged Buzzards, which may resemble the Steppe Buzzard (Plate 20, **9–11**) and dark Honey Buzzards (**3**). Confusion with the latter in adult plumage is unlikely, since it will show its classic tail-bands, but it may well persist with the rest even in the eyes of expert observers.

It must be stressed that buzzard identification is often made impossible by the distance, angle, or other circumstances of the observation. The best approach is to learn the commonest bird, the Buzzard, first and well. A full knowledge of its variations in silhouette and pattern greatly assist in the separation of the other buzzards and those other raptors, such as the Osprey and the smaller eagles, which also present chances for confusion. Fortunately the Buzzard remains relatively common and widespread and, when not persecuted, it often allows a quite close approach.

Among buzzards, it is the Honey Buzzard and the western and eastern forms of the Buzzard that form noticeable streams and large flocks when moving. Over particularly strong thermals the birds may form spectacular stacks with new arrivals joining at the bottom and onward departures made from the top. The movements of the Rough-legged and Long-legged Buzzards are much less visible, though both may gather in small groups at the end of a migration stage.

IW

22 Honey Buzzard *Pernis apivorus*
Buzzard *Buteo buteo*
Rough-legged Buzzard *Buteo lagopus*
Long-legged Buzzard *Buteo rufinus*

When perched, all buzzards show a fairly small-billed and -headed but full-bodied appearance. To an experienced eye and at close range, the kite-like form of the Honey Buzzard is discernible. The forepart of its head lacks the deep eye socket of *Buteo* and has an 'armour' of scale-like feathers.

The Honey Buzzard occupies wasp-filled woodlands in the West Palearctic, north to 67°N. A summer visitor with a total European population of at least 25 000 pairs, it streams south to the African forests by the traditional narrow strait routes. Typical birds (7) show greyer heads and backs and more boldly marked underparts than the 'true' *Buteo* buzzards. Dark birds (8) are very confusing.

The Buzzard ranges widely through the wilderness and wooded areas of the West Palearctic, being strongly migratory only in the north-east whence a well-marked race, the so-called Steppe Buzzard, moves south into Africa in winter. The total European population probably approaches 150 000 pairs and this is one of the few raptors that shows no general recent decline. The variation in its plumage is indicated here by a light bird (4) and a typical one (3).

The essentially arctic Rough-legged Buzzard preys on tundra animals and occasionally nests on low hummocks. Breeding mainly north of 65°N, it winters within 45° and 55°N, haunting particularly marshes and steppes. Its population fluctuates markedly, in a cycle allied to the population density of small mammals, and is unlikely to exceed 7000 pairs in the west Palearctic even in peak years. Typically it shows a white head and a white black-banded tail, with the adult (5) having black belly and thighs, less marked in the juvenile (6).

The largely resident Long-legged Buzzard inhabits arid habitats mainly in North Africa, south-east Europe, and Turkey. The total population is unmeasured and could well be below 1000 pairs. The typical adult (1) is a colourful bird, recalling the Steppe Buzzard, but with a paler tail. Dark birds (2) are very confusing but the strongly barred tail is striking.

23 Lesser Spotted Eagle *Aquila pomarina*
Spotted Eagle *Aquila clanga*

The spotted eagles are only so in immature plumage and then only markedly so in the larger species. Both are less impressive eagles than the other *Aquila* species, inhabiting old forests when breeding, and aquatic habitats in winter. They nest in trees.

The Lesser Spotted Eagle is more widespread in the West Palearctic than the Spotted, reaching west to 12°E. Its known breeding population is less than 900 pairs. The adult (1) is a dull brown bird with no striking feature; the juvenile (2) is similarly coloured, with white streaks on nape and underbody and bold white tips to greater coverts and secondaries.

The Spotted Eagle occurs nowhere east of 20°E but ranges as far north as 65°N in Russia. Some birds winter within the south-east of the West Palearctic. Its known breeding population does not exceed 1750 pairs. The adult (3) is a dark, sooty bird and the typical juvenile (4) is splendidly streaked and spotted on its body and wings. The pale morph juvenile (5) is confusing, suggesting the Tawny and Steppe Eagle and even the young Imperial Eagle (Plates 25 and 26).

The genus *Aquila*, often deemed to contain the 'true' eagles, is the penultimate group in the West Palearctic Accipitridae and together its members represent an undoubted climax to the size and strength of actively hunting raptors. There are at least six species. All are now relatively scarce or rare and local birds, with the chances that they offer for observation usually difficult to obtain Thus initially they are easily confused with *Buteo*, *Hieraaetus*, and even vultures, but with longer experience their structure and actions become much more recognizable and rarely fail to convey an extra degree of aerial majesty. All *Aquila* eagles are strong-billed, deep- and bold-eyed, powerful birds, with long wings and usually full, but not always long tails. Their primaries, when outstretched, are noticeably 'fingered' with six tips usually visible.

Looked at many times, the multiple images of eagles can be seen to vary and do so most constantly in total size, head set, wing shape, tail form, and wing attitude. Thus the Lesser Spotted Eagle (1–3) is a slighter, somewhat longer-necked, narrower-winged, and proportionately longer-tailed bird than the Spotted Eagle (4–9) and both are rather lighter in form than most other *Aquila* eagles, with faster wing-beats in active flight. The term 'ragged mats' has been applied to the (when fully extended) broad, six or seven 'fingered' wings of the Spotted Eagle, which may recall those of *Haliaeetus*, and its rather broad head can be distinguished at close range. Both species soar and glide on wings held flat next to the body but drooped beyond the carpal joint, particularly during the latter mode of flight. They can look noticeably bowed at a distance.

The term 'spotted eagle' comes from the much spotted plumage of the juvenile Spotted Eagle (9); it is far less relevant to the similarly aged Lesser Spotted Eagle (3) and both species lose any such pattern within two years of hatching. The other plumage marks of sub-adults are variable, overlapping with those of the similarly aged Imperial, Steppe, and Tawny Eagles (Plate 27). The most telling are the white inner primary bases of the Lesser Spotted Eagle (2 and 3), the reversed contrast of wing-lining and quills—respectively brown and black in the Lesser Spotted Eagle (1) and black and dark grey-brown in the Spotted Eagle (4 and 5)—and the lack of pale tips to the under greater coverts which create a diagnostic wing-bar on the Steppe and some Imperial Eagles (Plate 27, respectively 8, 10, and 3). The characteristic U-shaped white band above the tail in the two 'spotted eagles' is most obvious on immatures but may persist on adults. Unfortunately, not dissimilar marks occur also on several other eagles and they are not, therefore, diagnostic of any species. The only other widespread eagle as black-looking as the adult Spotted is the Imperial Eagle.

On migration, it is the Lesser Spotted Eagle that assembles in streams; exceptionally, up to 9000 birds may be seen on one day at favourable migration points. Thus any group of 'spotted eagles' is likely to be of that species and not the (in Europe) much scarcer and more solitary Spotted Eagle.

25 Tawny and Steppe Eagle *Aquila rapax*
Verreaux's Eagle *Aquila verreauxii*

The magnificent Verreaux's Eagle has tried to breed in Israel since 1961, in an almost bewildering extension of its essentially East African range. The adult (**5**) is the only truly jet-black eagle, with its white braces and lower back often concealed at rest. The juvenile (**6**) is noticeably variegated in appearance, with its black underparts contrasting with pale crown, rusty mantle, and beautifully scaled wing-coverts.

The Tawny and Steppe Eagles are here regarded as forming two groups of subspecies, though some prefer to regard the Steppe Eagle group as forming a separate species. The former group contains, for *Aquila*, rather small sluggish birds, content at times to eat amphibians and to scavenge. Its north-west African population is now tiny. The Steppe Eagle group includes distinctly larger and more active birds, as closely resembling the Imperial Eagle in form and behaviour as they do the Tawny.

Its western range approaches the Black Sea, and the European population perhaps numbers some tens of pairs. At close range, the length of the yellow gape is a helpful mark, with that of the Steppe extending noticeably further to behind the eye. The adult Steppe Eagle (**1**) is darker, lacking the obvious pale nape of other *Aquila* eagles and the contrasting, darker quills of the Tawny (**3**); the juvenile (**2**) is warmer brown than the Tawny (**4**). Few northern Tawny Eagles are quite as pale as those shown, which resemble the birds of African populations.

It must be stressed that the Tawny and Steppe Eagles also present many chances for confusion or mistaken identifications with their congeners, since at different ages they resemble not only the Imperial Eagle but also the Spotted and Lesser Spotted Eagles. Flight characters (Plate 27) are also subject to overlap.

26 Imperial Eagle *Aquila heliaca*
Golden Eagle *Aquila chrysaetos*

When perched, like the other *Aquila* eagles, these two majestic eagles usually adopt fairly horizontal postures unlike those of the fish eagles, and their deep-billed, rather long heads, and shaggy 'trousers' are always obvious. The Imperial Eagle nests mainly in mature trees whereas the Golden Eagle prefers cliff-ledges.

The Imperial Eagle is restricted in the west Palearctic to Iberia and the south-east of the region, south of 55°N and east of 17°E. Much decreased, its population is now seriously threatened and can only muster about 200 pairs outside Russia. The isolated Spanish population is down to about 60 pairs. The northern birds of the eastern communities move south in winter. The adult eagle is a very dark eagle, with both

races showing a very pale crown and shawl, and the Spanish birds (**3**) a white forewing as well as the white braces of the eastern birds (**1**). The juvenile of the latter (**2**) is well streaked and spotted, recalling the Spotted Eagle, but its ground colour is much paler.

The Golden Eagle is the most widespread and most sedentary of all the eagles, inhabiting montane areas across almost the entire longitudes and latitudes of the West Palearctic. Of the 2600 or so known pairs east of Russia, the most secure 300 are in Scotland, and their young have tried to reoccupy both Ireland and England. The gold of the adult (**4**) is obvious on the crown, nape, and across the central wing-coverts.

The genus *Aquila* contains one very confusing species, the systematically awkward Tawny and Steppe Eagle, with its double English name indicating its two racial groups which are lumped in scientific terms as, respectively, the nominate *rapax* group and the *nipalensis* group. Individual populations range from the small, scruffy Tawny Eagles of north-west Africa to the large, well-ordered Steppe Eagles of eastern Europe, and their structure and actions vary correspondingly. Thus the Tawny (Plate 28, **9**) is noticeably less impressive on the wing than the Steppe (**6–10**) whose flight silhouette appearance is much closer to that of the Imperial Eagle. Even so, every *Aquila rapax* shows a rather heavy and clumsy flight action, with wings held level when soaring and often held loosely—with crooked outline—when gliding. With a sudden switch of behaviour, they may change to piratical hunting around a carrion source. One structural character is diagnostic in flight: the inner primaries of *A. rapax* are noticeably shorter than those of their congeners, and give the outer wing a characteristically pinched look, particularly marked in the juvenile (**10**) with its pale-tipped inner quills. The Imperial Eagle also holds its wings flat and shows a more protruding head and a slightly shorter tail than the Golden Eagle.

At close range and in good light, the adult *A. rapax* is a dark brown eagle and shows little plumage relief except, against strong light, closely barred and greyer quills and tail. In contrast, the sub-adult Steppe Eagle is markedly multi-coloured, with a pattern not unlike the 'spotted' eagles but differing in the huge white areas on the inner primaries when juvenile (**9**), and the obvious pale border to its wing-lining when immature (**8** and **10**). The adult Imperial Eagle is brown-black and shows a noticeably pale crown and nape, a grey tail-base (**1**) and, in addition, white 'fore arms' in its Spanish form (not shown). In contrast, the sub-adult Imperial Eagle recalls both the young *A. rapax* and the confusing pale morph of the Spotted Eagle (Plate 24, **6**). The best marks of the young Imperial Eagle are its bold white rump and pale notch on the inner primaries when juvenile (**3** and **5**) and the partly buff-brown body and under greater coverts of the immature (**3**). It is also important to remember that the Imperial Eagle is larger and more majestic than the 'spotted' and the Steppe Eagles.

It is quite exceptional for the Imperial Eagle and the Tawny Eagle to appear overhead other than as single birds, though the latter may form small groups around a food source. The Steppe Eagle can appear in streams, including loose parties that may stack with other numerous raptors in thermals.

It should be noted that in spite of all the observations made on migrant eagles of all ages in the last quarter century, the last word on their identification remains difficult to write.

The genus *Aquila* contains two species that combine to an unusual degree both power and grace. They are the Golden Eagle and the Verreaux's Eagle, the largest members of the genus in the West Palearctic, where the former is the most widespread *Aquila* eagle, while the latter is the most restricted. Both are relatively long-tailed eagles but their wing structure differs distinctly. That of the Golden Eagle is buzzard-like, but with noticeably greater length, more widely 'fingered' primaries, and a distinctive, shallow S outline to the trailing edge. That of the Verreaux's Eagle is quite different, with a noticeably narrow base, marked central breadth and thus overall a somewhat leaf-like shape. Both species soar on noticeably raised wings, set in a position similar to that adopted by the Buzzard, and glide on slightly raised or flat wings. Their wing-beats are deep and powerful but both species usually indulge in only short periods of flapping flight, such is their mastery of soaring and planing flight.

Even at a distance, the plumages of these eagles are usually distinctive. Thus the adult Golden Eagle (**1** and **2**) is a rich brown with a gold crown and nape and bold yellowish or cream panels over the upper wing-coverts. The immature Golden Eagle (**3** and **4**) has a striking white wing-panel and a basally white and distally black tail, recalling that of the Rough-legged Buzzard. The adult Verreaux's Eagle is an essentially black eagle, its plumage strikingly relieved by a broad, pale patch over its primaries (**5** and **6**) and its white braces, back, and rump (**6**). The immature Verreaux's Eagle (**7** and **8**) is also strikingly patterned, sharing only the primary patches of its adult and being otherwise noticeably more buzzard-like in its pattern (**7**) than any other young eagle.

The juvenile Tawny Eagle (**9**) lacks the pale rear border to the wing-lining that is so typical of the Steppe Eagle (Plate 27, **8** – **10**). Its relatively weak appearance is worth repetition, for it is the most insignificant bird of a magnificent tribe. It is typical of all three eagles discussed above to appear singly in the sky, whatever their behaviour. The rule is only broken by young birds during the early period of their dispersal.

All the *Aquila* eagles may, at long range, invite confusion with other large raptors from vultures to other eagles and buzzards. Sadly few are easily observed and to achieve experience of them in summer, long journeys to wildernesses and careful stalking are required. In spring and autumn their passages are noticeably concentrated over narrow straits, and it is from watches of these that most modern knowledge of their form and appearance has come. Once learnt, it is one of the chief birdwatching prizes.

1

2

3

4

5

6

7

8

9

IW

The so-called hawk-eagles *Hieraaetus* make up a widespread and varied group in the southern parts of the Old World, but only two occur in the West Palearctic, following the true eagles in systematic order. All three species shown opposite are medium-sized to quite large raptors, with long wings and long tails. The Booted Eagle has, however, a particularly confusing appearance, at times recalling *Buteo* buzzards and *Milvus* kites, but the Bonelli's Eagle has a distinctive character. The Osprey is the only member of the genus *Pandion*; it is distinctive in many ways and is often called the 'Fish-hawk'.

The flight action of both *Hieraaetus* eagles is frequently swift, agile, and—in the Bonelli's—noticeably powerful. The Booted Eagle soars persistently with wings held flat and glides with lowered primaries; it frequently twists its tail in the manner of a kite. The Bonelli's soars less than any other eagle on flat or slightly raised wings and usually intersperses flat- and bunched-winged glides with loose but not deep wing-beats. Its climbs and stoops in display are very impressive. The flight action of the Osprey is noticeably loose, with the shallow but powerful beats of its long wings often recalling a large gull. Its soaring attitude is distinctive, with wings raised on the inner half but lowered on the outer and thus appearing noticeably bowed. Its head may protrude in an upwards curve. When diving for fish, the Osprey may briefly hover first or, more usually, end a long approach 'spy-glide' with a shallow, feet-first plunge.

In good light, the plumage marks of *Hieraaetus* and *Pandion* are more obvious than those of most raptors. Above, the adult Bonelli's Eagle (**1**) has a striking pale patch on the mantle and a dark-tipped, grey tail; the pale morph Booted Eagle (**5**) shows noticeably cream central wing-coverts and upper tail-coverts; and the Osprey presents a white crown and noticeably barred tail. Below, plumage patterns vary more, with a marked age progression in the Bonelli's Eagle and dimorphism in the Booted Eagle to be considered. Thus the Bonelli's changes from a noticeably rufous juvenile (**4**), with a thin black border to its wing-lining and faintly barred tail, through a darker, brown sub-adult (**3**) to an essentially black, grey, and white adult (**2**), with its uniquely contrasting black wing-lining and white body. The pale morph Booted Eagle (**6**) may be confused with the Egyptian Vulture at great height but the longer, square tail of the eagle should prevent a lasting mistake. The dark morph (**7**) is very troublesome, inviting confusion with the Black Kite, the Marsh Harrier, and melanistic buzzards. The pale rufous-pink tail is its most helpful character, as the faintly paler inner primaries do not always show.

From below, the Osprey (**9**) presents a noticeably white wing-lining and body, and the relief of black primary 'fingers', carpal patches, and greater coverts and grey-banded quills and tail is striking, though suggesting pale morph buzzards at times.

Of these birds, only the Booted Eagles regularly move in streams among other soaring raptors on migration, but their passages are rarely more than thin, with the sight of more than a handful in touch with each other uncommon. The scarce Osprey occasionally passes in coastal processions but usually it and the Bonelli's Eagle appear as single birds.

30 Bonelli's Eagle *Hieraaetus fasciatus*
Booted Eagle *Hieraaetus pennatus*
Osprey *Pandion haliaetus*

The medium-sized, long-tailed Bonelli's Eagle somewhat recalls a pale Honey Buzzard. Its West Palearctic stongholds are Spain and north-west Africa, where about 550 sedentary pairs nest on cliff-ledges and in fissures and trees. The adult (**1**) has a diagnostic white patch on the back and well streaked, white underparts. The juvenile (**2**) is very different, with a rufous hue to its plumage.

The much smaller Booted Eagle recalls both the *Buteo* buzzards and the *Milvus* kites. Largely sympatric with the Bonelli's Eagle in the west, it extends further north to 55°N in the east. Its western Palearctic population exceeds 9500 pairs, which nest in trees. It migrates to Africa in winter. The Booted Eagle is strikingly dimorphic, with the dark morph (**3**) and even the pale one (**4**) suggesting several other species. The wing pattern is, however, characteristic, with its three, almost even, bands of colour.

The unique Osprey is dependent on fish-bearing waters and is commonest in the northern taiga, though there are scattered coastal and island communities elsewhere. The threatened European population hardly exceeds 1400 pairs, nesting mainly on trees and most migrate to Africa in winter. Its return as a Scottish breeding bird has been a triumph of practical conservation. The juvenile (**6**) shows distinctly scaled upperparts, unlike the adult (**5**). The loose, long-winged form of a perched Osprey is always striking.

31 Lesser Kestrel *Falco naumanni*
Kestrel *Falco tinnunculus*
American Kestrel *Falco sparverius*

The Lesser Kestrel has a slimmer build, narrower wings, and more slender tail than the Kestrel. In the West Palearctic, its dependence on large insect prey makes it uncommon and local except in Iberia and east of 20°E. Hole-nesting, it breeds in colonies of 15–25 pairs. In sharp decline almost everywhere in Europe, its main stronghold is in Spain, where there may still be 50 000 pairs. Except in southern areas, it is a long-distance migrant, wintering south of the Sahara. The adult male (**1**) shows no moustache, no spots on the back, but has much blue-grey on the wing-coverts; the female (**2**) is less heavily marked than the Kestrel (**7**). Both show diagnostic pale claws at close range. The sub-adult male (**3**) presents a very dangerous pitfall in kestrel identification, with its Kestrel-like back and wing pattern.

The Kestrel is the commonest and best known diurnal raptor in most of the West Palearctic, usually nesting in holes. It is predominantly sedentary as an adult in west and south-central Europe but highly migratory at all ages in Fenno-Scandia and Russia. The male (**3**) shows a distinctly spotted back and inner wing; the female Kestrel (**7**) shows heavy moustaches, heavy body streaks, and pronounced barring over the wings and back.

The American Kestrel, which has crossed the Atlantic to the Azores, Britain, Denmark, and Malta, is distinctly smaller, with an intricate and colourful head pattern. The adult male (**4**) is strongly rufous from back to tail, with a contrasting, rather dark blue-grey inner wing. The female (**5**) is more intensely coloured than the female Kestrel (**7**), with a bay rump and tail.

32 Red-footed Falcon *Falco vespertinus*
Amur Falcon *Falco amurensis*

The Red-footed Falcon is a small, fairly compact falcon, with a character and plumage patterns that recall both the Kestrel and the Hobby. In the West Palearctic it is confined as a breeding bird to the wooded steppe and open taiga east of 17°E and betwen 45° and 63°N. On migration it frequently strays west, particularly on its spring return from south-west Africa. Outside Russia, its population does not much exceed 700 pairs which breed usually in old crow nests. The adult cock (1) is dark blue-slate, with rufous vent and red bare parts; its silvery-edged primaries are already shown by the sub-adult male (3), which has parti-coloured underparts and a strikingly pale throat. The juvenile (5) can be confused with the Hobby but is more broadly scaled and browner, especially on the crown. The immature female (4) lacks the grey-and-black-barred back and fully orange body, nape, and crown of the adult hen (2).

The Amur or Manchurian Red-footed Falcon, the eastern Asiatic relative of the Red-footed, could well stray to Europe. Both the adult male (6) and the female (7) show white wing-linings, but these are less distinct on sub-adults.

As indicated, both species have more complex and sexually distinct plumage progressions than any other falcon. A full understanding of these can be acquired by the reading of fuller texts, such as those in the plumage sections of volume II of *The Birds of the Western Palearctic*.

33 Hobby *Falco subbuteo*
Merlin *Falco columbarius*

Always elegant, the rather slight Hobby is the widest ranging and most migratory of all falcons. From winter haunts in southern Africa, it invades most of the wooded West Palearctic from 32° to 67°N and from 8°W, shunning only the north-west maritime periphery of Europe. Outside Russia, the known population probably reaches 9000 pairs which breed in old crow and other large nests in trees. The adult (1) is beautifully marked, with its contrasting moustache and pale throat catching the eye more than its rufous thighs and vent or striped body. The juvenile (2) shows the basic plumage pattern well, but lacks the rufous vent. It can prompt confusion with the Red-footed, Eleonora's, and Sooty Falcons.

Gram for gram the most power-packed falcon, the rather compact Merlin is a bird of open heathy habitats along the coasts of and in the interior of Europe north of 50°N. Thus it is the most arctic of the small falcons, usually nesting on the ground. Its population has been little measured but there may be 5000 pairs in Ireland, Britain, and Fenno-Scandia. The adult male (3) is a quite pale, colourful bird, essentially grey-blue above and pink-buff below. The female (4) and juvenile (5) are difficult to tell apart, with dark brown upperparts, heavily streaked underbodies, and boldly barred tails. The pale nape is usually larger on the juvenile. Once known, the Merlin is one of the easiest falcons to identify.

As indicated, both these species have less complex plumage progressions than the other falcons.

34 Eleonora's Falcon *Falco eleonorae*
Sooty Falcon *Falco concolor*

The Eleonora's Falcon is the most attenuated and therefore the most rakish of all falcons. Its breeding range is the most restricted of the family and encompasses only island and coastal crags from the Canary Islands through the Mediterranean to Cyprus, among which are scattered the total world population of about 4500 pairs. The bird rears one brood, usually in cliff nests, during the autumn migration of passerines which form the bulk of its prey. It winters in East Africa and Madagascar and only rarely overshoots its limits on migration. twice reaching Britain. The adult may be dark-slate overall (2) or only above, with its streaked rufous underbody and pale cheeks and throat (1) tending to suggest the Hobby, as does the paler juvenile (3).

The Sooty Falcon is rather smaller and shorter-tailed than the Eleonora's, but its form is still elegant. Like the Eleonora's, it preys on migrant birds but in desert, not marine habitats, being well-established in the West Palearctic only in Libya and Egypt. Its total population is unknown, but it accompanies the Eleonora's Falcon to Madagascar, where over 10 000 birds have been estimated to winter, and others have been seen then in parts of East Africa. The light, grey morph (4) is much the commonest; the dark, slate one (5) is difficult to tell from the larger Eleonora's, except when the characteristic extension of the central tail-feathers is evident. The juvenile (6) has a noticeably clouded chest and the ground colour of the underparts is colder than those of Eleonora's and Hobby.

35 Lanner *Falco biarmicus*
Saker *Falco cherrug*

The Lanner is a medium-sized but still rather rakish falcon, which recalls both the pale morph Eleonora's Falcon and the Peregrine but lacks the latter's power. It haunts warm, open plains and mountainsides and is confined to the Mediterranean region and the African savannas. Its European population is in a perilous state, numbering probably only about 50 pairs. It is widespread in Africa, but numbers are unknown. It breeds in the old nests of other crag-nesting birds. The adult of North African and Levantine populations (3) is noticeably paler grey above than that of the Balkan communities (1) but both show the specific rufous crown and distinctly spotted white underparts. The juvenile (2) is darker than the adult, with a chestnut crown and heavily streaked body, and invites confusion with both the Peregrine and the Saker.

The Saker is a heavy-headed, large, robust falcon, exceeding both the Lanner and Peregrine in bulk. It is another plains-haunting raptor of middle latitudes in the West Palearctic, breeding north to 56°N. Some winter as far south as the equator but others concentrate in the northern deserts of the Levant. The Saker breeds in old nests on crags and trees. Outside Russia, the east European population is probably under 150 pairs and declining in some areas. The Saker is always a brown and white falcon, with a noticeably white crown in the adult (4) and a white-streaked crown and very heavily splashed underparts in the juvenile (5). Its moustache is less pronounced than that of the Lanner. Confusion with the darker Gyrfalcons has to be avoided.

36 Gyrfalcon *Falco rusticolus*

The Gyrfalcon haunts the Arctic as majestically as the Polar Bear, and shows more weight and power than any congener. It is a bird of coasts, river valleys, and montane crags in the far north of Europe, Asia, and North America, hunting birds in the main and breeding in old nests on ledges or (rarely) in trees. Mainly due to direct human persecution, it is seriously endangered everywhere in Europe, with perhaps only about 300 pairs remaining. All adults range north of 60°N in summer and even their young rarely stray south of 50°N in winter. Adult plumage is variable, being usually described in three morphs, the white (**1**) almost unmarked except for a few marks concentrated above, the intermediate (**2**) dark but still greyer and more uniformly patterned than the Peregrine, and the dark (**3**) very black, with its moustaches pronounced but still lacking the barred underparts of the Peregrine. The juveniles are more heavily marked, the difference being more obvious in the white morph (**4**) than the dark (**5**).

37 Peregrine *Falco peregrinus*
Barbary Falcon *Falco pelegrinoides*

The Peregrine, which has a scattered but almost world-wide distribution, is the third largest falcon of the West Palearctic. Once widespread there north of 55°N, persecution, toxic chemicals, disturbance, and theft of young have reduced its population to a scattered shadow of its former self, with its remaining strongholds in Britain, France, Spain, and Turkey. It has declined markedly also in North America, largely due to pesticide poisoning. North-eastern birds migrate south and west in winter. The adult male Peregrine is a black-headed, broadly moustached bird, with well barred underparts; the typical northern European bird (**1**) is less buff below than the Spanish (**4**) but less pale and less grey above than the north Russian (**5**). The adult female is larger than the male and more heavily barred below, particularly on the flanks and thighs; the juveniles (**2** and **3**, both females) are much browner than the adult, with heavy spots appearing as lines on its underparts.

The Barbary Falcon is a small edition of the Peregrine, occurring mostly inland in arid regions south of the range of the Peregrine and breeding in similar niches. In the West Palearctic, it is distinctly local in occurrence and is confined to North Africa, Sinai, and Israel. In these areas the population density is variable, but the total cannot exceed more than a few hundred pairs. Compared to the typical (northern) Peregrine, it is a paler, greyer bird, with its size varying less between male (**6**) and female (**7**) and with its rear crown and nape pale at all ages, being buff to chestnut in the adult (**6**, **7**, and the eastern form **9**) and brown-white in the juvenile (**8**). The marks on the underparts are indistinct, notably so in the male (**6**) but also in the brown juvenile (**8**).

The Falconidae represent, along with the smaller members of the Accipitridae, the most active and agile of birds of prey. Systematically it is the last family of the order and is generally regarded as being, size for size and mien for mien, the most impressive. All small falcons lack real bulk but possess great character, with relatively broad, round heads, long pointed wings, and proportionately long tails combining in a distinctive multiple image that conveys vigour, momentum and purpose. This is particularly obvious in flight, when a burst of fluid, yet clipped wing-beats provides yet more dash, or a float of outstretched wings allows a sudden circle, or a burst of wing-beats holds the bird still in an accomplished hover, the last action being most persistently evident in the two kestrels. Of the five species shown here, the Kestrel is the most distinctive, since in many areas it is the only hovering small falcon and is usually relatively tame. The Merlin is the most fierce, its hunting skills including a most dramatic 'chase and snatch' often employed against the smaller birds of summer heaths and winter coasts and farmland. The Red-footed Falcon is the most insectivorous, its abilities including aerial feeding on dusk-flying moths and beetles.

The plumage patterns of small falcons vary considerably, with marked sexual differences in all species and complex age progressions in some. Adult males are fairly easy to tell apart, with the Lesser Kestrel (3) distinguished from the Kestrel (1) by the blue-grey panel on its larger wing-coverts, the American Kestrel (11) unique in having a solidly chestnut back and tail, the Merlin (9) being strikingly grey-blue, and the Red-footed Falcon (5) totally slate except for its silvery quills. In the case of females and immatures, identification is much more difficult. There is no certain way to tell the Lesser Kestrel (4) from the Kestrel (2), except by the more pointed tail-centre (when it shows) and the grey rump (on some birds) of the former; and only the head pattern, bay rump, and small size—not always discernible in a brief view—distinguish the American Kestrel (2). The young or hen Merlin (10) is easier, with its darker brown plumage—noticeably pale banded on the fanned tail—usually obvious in good light, but the similarly sexed and aged Red-footed Falcon (6–8) is distinctly confusing, with an initial plumage pattern (8) reminiscent of the Hobby (Plate 38, 8) giving way to a slate-blue sub-adult male phase (7) or an orange-headed, grey-black female (6). In all these plumages, the Red-footed shows a strongly barred tail and the grey and black cross-barring of the female's back (6) is unique in West Palearctic falcons.

Of these delightful birds, two species appear characteristically in groups. They are the Lesser Kestrel and the Red-footed Falcon. When over the African savannas, their loose migrant assemblies may join into flocks of thousands. The abundant Kestrel shows only a tendency to move in thin processions but on migration may form loose flocks. The scarce Merlin whips past on its own.

IW

In the five species shown here, size varies considerably, from the fairly small Hobby and Sooty Falcon, through the very long-winged Eleonora's Falcon, to the quite large Lanner, and the even larger Saker. Like the small falcons, all are long-winged and long-tailed birds with a sleek, slim form in the first three but more robustness and bulk in the last two. All are swift and powerful fliers, fully capable of taking fast-flying insects and birds in the air, but no falcons are more graceful than the Hobby and the Eleonora's whose slow easy wing-beats in patrol flight suddenly quicken to send the birds into headlong pursuit or ferocious stoops. The Sooty Falcon has much of the majesty of these two but holds its wings more acutely angled in normal flight. The Lanner is also graceful, lacking the full weight of the Saker and other large falcons (Plate 40), but its wings are relatively broader, giving a more rowing, less scything wing-beat. The most distinctive flight silhouette is the attenuated cruciform shape of the Eleonora's Falcon.

The sexual differences and plumage progressions of medium-sized falcons are less complex than those of small falcons but all go through a somewhat paler, browner juvenile dress before attaining the more immaculate adult appearance. This rule is subject to racial and other variations, however, and great care is required in all field identifications. Thus the east European Lanner (**1**) is much bluer or slatier above than the North African and Levantine form (**3**) and both races have a drab brown juvenile (**2**). The pale warm-coloured crown of the adult (**1** and **3**) is ditinctive but this character can also be shown by the Barbary Falcon (Plate 40). From above, the Hobby and the Eleonora's Falcon look very similar though the juvenile Hobby (**8**) can show a pale nape and a scalier back at close range. Its lack of obvious tail barring distinguishes it from the young Red-footed (Plate 39). The adult Sooty Falcon (**9**) is typically dull grey; its juvenile (**10**) is drabber and browner. Both look relatively uniform in colour and lack the bright white cheeks of the Hobby and the light morph Eleonora's (**6**). The dark morph adult Eleonora's Falcon (**5**) is exceptionally dark slate and is only separable from the dark morph of the Sooty Falcon (not shown here) by size and structure, notably the point in the end of the folded tail of the latter.

Of all the species shown here, only the Lanner is likely to be confused with the most widespread of all falcons, the Peregrine. The darker, bluer birds are especially confusing but even they do not exhibit the powerful flight of the Peregrine. The Saker (**3** and **4**) is more fully discussed against the next plate. The birds shown here are pale morphs.

Of these falcons, only the breeding Eleonora's regularly appear in the sky in small groups, and on migration in Africa, it, the Hobby, and the Sooty may all join in the same loose stream. The Lanner and the Saker are usually seen singly.

All four species shown here are bulky, quite large to huge falcons, showing much greater power than the rest of the Falconidae and fully capable of knocking down mammals and striking large birds out of the sky. Their grace tends to diminish as their size increases and the largest, the Gyrfalcon, may even suggest a large *Accipiter* hawk or buzzard at times. Like the Lanner, their flight action is usually less scything and more rowing in patrolling flight but it becomes much more rapid and skilful in pursuit of prey, with both 'chase and strike' and 'dive and strike' techniques employed. The latter, also known as stooping, is most constantly employed in the Peregrine, hence its very high value as a falconer's bird. The former is most obvious in the Saker and the Gyrfalcon, whose horizontal momentum can be awesome to a human observer (and presumably to their prey). At times when they are patrolling, the flight actions of all these species recall those of the Fulmar.

Plumage patterns vary as in other falcons; potential confusions abound and only the white (**1**) and intermediate (**2**) morphs of the Gyrfalcon are easy to identify. The dark morph Gyrfalcon (**3**) has to be distinguished from the darker Sakers and the largest Peregrines. It rarely looks brown in any light. The best marks of the Saker are the noticeably white-spotted tail (**4** and **5**) and the white crown of the old adult (**4**). It should be noted that its brown plumage tones overlap with those of the Lanner (Plate 39) and that even experts can fail to distinguish them in the field.

The problems of separating the Peregrine (**6–8**) from the Barbary (**9** and **10**) are considerable. Not all systematists agree that they are full species and the small Iberian race of the Peregrine (not shown here) is very close in appearance to the Barbary, even showing a rufous nape. The best chances lie with the patterns of their under plumage, size, and form. A pale, noticeably blue-grey 'Peregrine' is always worth a second look. In the south, it may be a Barbary; in the north, it could be an eastern Peregrine from Russia and Siberia (Plate 37, **5**).

For many raptor enthusiasts, these superb falcons rival the true eagles and the rarer vultures in class. The enjoyment that they provide is immense and their accomplished mode of hunting is the most impressive of all birds of prey. Small wonder that falconers prize them so highly. Would that all would recognize their increasing rarity and leave them to their own haunts.

Other than over their breeding grounds, it is quite exceptional for these falcons to associate in the same area of sky. All typically present solitary images of power and momentum, and even their partial migrations are only rarely detectable in the thinnest of aerial streams.

With the exception of the always-colourful Red-footed Falcon, the undersides of small falcons present no really striking plumage patterns and the quick recognition of their differences comes only from long practice. Once again, the kestrels are difficult to tell apart, with the Kestrel, the hen or immature Lesser Kestrel, and the American Kestrel all showing a basically similar colour ground and pattern of streaks and bars. The most helpful marks are the relatively large and heavy spots of the Kestrel, especially in the hen and immature (**2**); the pointed tail-centre of the Lesser Kestrel (**3** and **4**) and the pale body ground of the American Kestrel (**6**). The strikingly white, black-edged underwing of the male Lesser (**3**) is very different from that of the male Kestrel (**1**)—but observers must beware the effect of odd lights which may conceal the true patterns— and the heavily spotted and barred underwing of the male American Kestrel (**5**) is also distinctive. In addition, the last shows against the light a subterminal line of translucent spots inside the tips of its quills (not shown here), which is less striking but also visible on the hen and immature (**6**).

Compared to the kestrels, the plumages of the Merlin (**11** and **12**) are noticeably dark below, with heavily barred wings, a streaked body, and a boldly banded tail. The pink-buff tone of the male's body (**11**) can glow strongly. It should be noted that the Merlin flies at a persistently lower level than any of the other small falcons.

The underside patterns of the Red-footed Falcon progress from an initially common, somewhat Kestrel-like dress (**10**)—but note the stronger quill and tail barring— to the strongly orange female (**8**) or to the multicoloured sub-adult male (**9**) and the slate and black adult male (**7**). On the last two, the characteristic rufous vent may show in good light as the birds perform hunting manoeuvres, but it often remains shaded in level flight. Among the small falcons, the Red-footed Falcon makes a specialty of dusk-feeding upon insects.

Because of their quickness in the air, the silhouettes of small falcons are not easy to separate. The bluntest wing-tip and longest body and tail belong to the Kestrel, the slimmest body and narrowest and most pointed tail to the Lesser Kestrel, and the roundest body and most frequently fanned tail to the active, often jinking Merlin. Once learnt, these are all helpful characters, as is the rather Hobby-like form of the Red-footed Falcon and the relative compactness of the American Kestrel when compared to its Old World cousins. None of these is invariable, however. In brief views at acute angles, small falcons can even look like small hawks and vice versa. So the one that is glimpsed soaring over a far wood could be either!

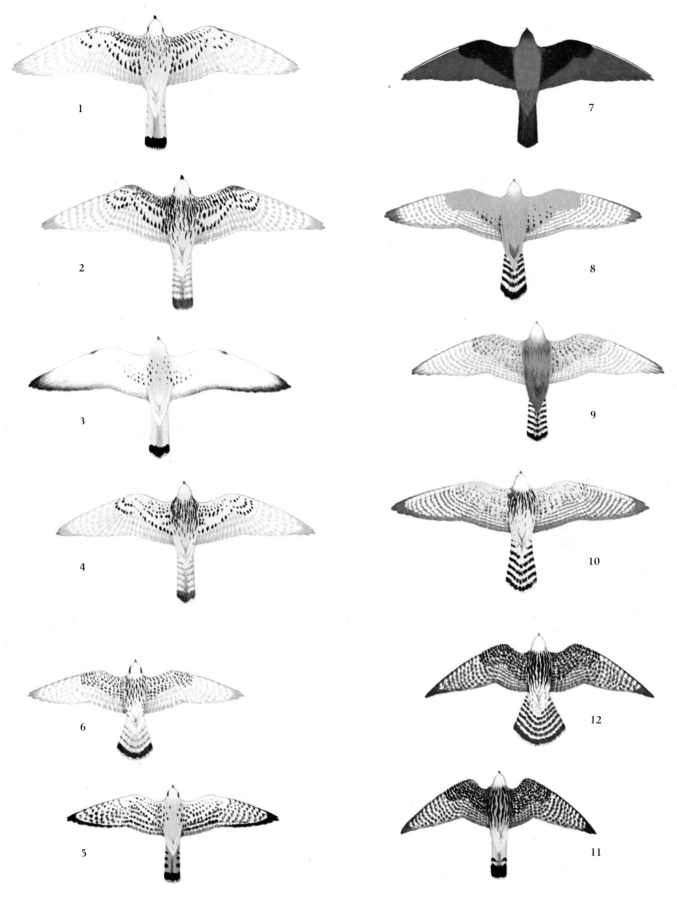

1W

Unlike most small falcons, their medium-sized brethren shown here do exhibit obvious plumage patterns on their undersides. The most striking is that of the adult dark morph Eleonora's Falcon (**5**) and Sooty Falcon (Plate 34, **5**), which apart from the lack of a rufous vent is similar to that of the smaller, less long-winged and -tailed adult male Red-footed Falcon (Plate 41, **7**). The most diagnostic are those of the typical Sooty, strikingly uniform in the adult (**7**) and only softly marked in the juvenile (**8**); the adult Hobby (**9**), with its very pale throat and rufous vent respectively placed fore and aft of its well streaked body and heavily barred underwing; and the juvenile Eleonora's Falcon (**6**), with its dark chestnut wing-lining and dark trailing wing-edge. The most confusing are those of the light morph adult Eleonora's Falcon (**4**), its body pattern somewhat recalling Hobby but with the underwing preventing a lasting mistake; and the juvenile Hobby (**10**), with its lack of a rufous vent giving a hint of the Merlin and the Red-footed Falcon (Plate 41, respectively **12** and **10**) and this only quickly cancelled out by its flight and behaviour.

The Lanner differs from the above three species not just in size but in the pale undersurface of the adult (**1** and **2**). The juvenile Lanner is very heavily marked on the wing-lining and body, looking much blacker there than the similarly aged Eleonora's. It is, however, dangerously similar to the young Saker (Plate 43, **8**).

Other differences between the medium-sized falcons are only discernible with practice. The most useful are structural. Thus the blunter wing-tip of the Lanner (**1–3**) is helpful, since the Hobby and the Eleonora's and Sooty Falcons have the most pointed wing-tips of their group. The Lanner is also the broadest winged, particularly in comparison to the Eleonora's and Sooty Falcons whose long, dark wings look very narrow at times. The longest tail belongs to the Eleonora's Falcon; the shortest is shown by the Hobby, which can briefly resemble a slim Peregrine at certain angles.

Of all the falcons that haunt the upper airspaces, the three smallest of the species shown here are the most constantly active and their silhouettes and behaviour may recall those of the other aerial feeding birds. Flying fast enough to catch hirundines, the Hobby is often compared to the Swift. It certainly cuts a similar arc across the sky but for sheer excitement, the hurtling dive of an Eleonora's Falcon along a Mediterranean cliff is unbeatable. Conversely, the Lanner often hunts at low level, and, in spite of its light form, it can fail to be as impressive in flight as its relatives.

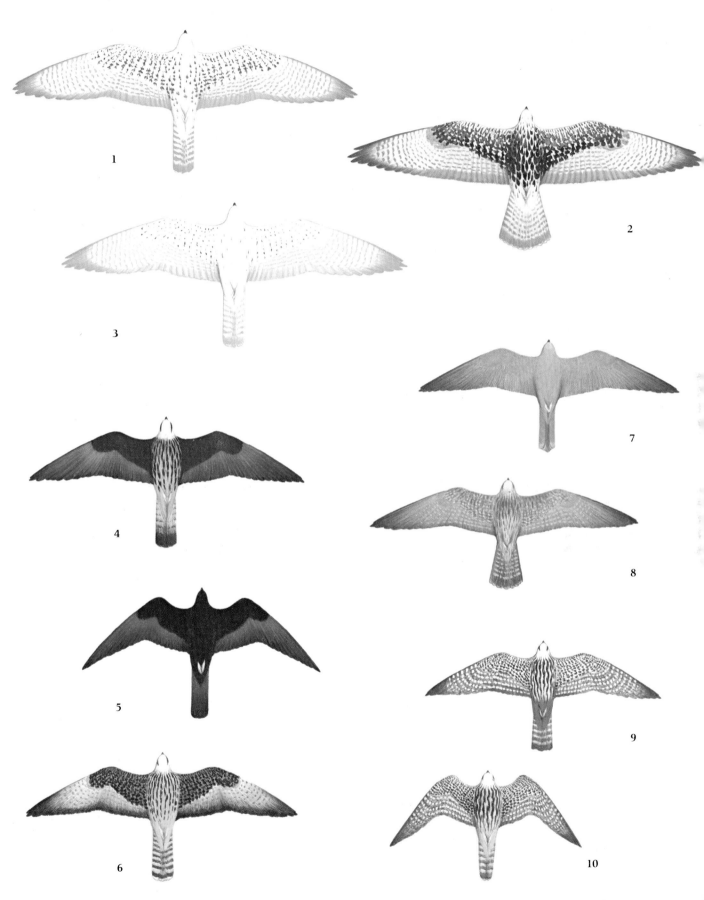

1

2

3

4

5

6

7

8

9

10

Among the largest falcons, the plumage patterns of their undersides show again the confusing overlaps so typical of their smallest relatives. Thus while the white morph (**1**) and dark morph (**3**) Gyrfalcon are respectively far too pale and far too dark for confusion to occur, all other plumages of the five species are full of pitfalls. Some adult Peregrines (not shown here) and most adult Sakers (**6**) and Barbary Falcons (**9**) look pale-bodied and the buff-pink wash of the last does not show in all lights. Most adult Peregrines (**8**) show, however, an isolated white throat and heavy barring over the wing-lining and lower body, a pattern quite unlike the normally faint marks on the Barbary Falcon (**9**), and the spots or streaks of the Saker (**6** and **7**). The last may also show a dark band across the wing-centre but such a mark is not diagnostic, as it appears on the Lanner (Plate 42) and even some Gyrfalcons (**2**). The intermediate morph Gyrfalcon (**2**) is easily confused with the largest female Peregrines, particularly when it sports obvious moustaches. Dark wing-tips are a feature common to these magnificent raptors. They are most pronounced in the Gyrfalcon and Saker and least so in the Barbary Falcon.

All immatures of the five species shown here are streaked on the body, heavily so in the Gyrfalcon (not shown here) and Saker (**8**), copiously on most Peregrines (**5**), but only lightly on the Barbary Falcon (**10**).

Structural differences in the largest falcons can be helpful. Thus the Gyrfalcon has the fullest tail, the broadest wings, and the bluntest wing-tip, with these features even suggesting a pale Buzzard when combined with the slow wing-beats of its patrolling flight. The flight form of the Saker is intermediate between those of the Gyrfalcon and the Peregrine but it never has quite the compactness of the latter. The Barbary Falcon is the most compact of all, looking at times like a Fulmar. It should be noted that of these falcons, it is typical of the two smaller species to ascend to greater heights than the larger two and the Lanner, all of which tend to patrol the lower airspace.

At all times these falcons look bulky and heavy in flight, unlike the other members of the family. This appearance adds to their overall momentum which is unmatched in all other raptors in the West Palearctic and is proved by their ability to kill prey outright by a strike.

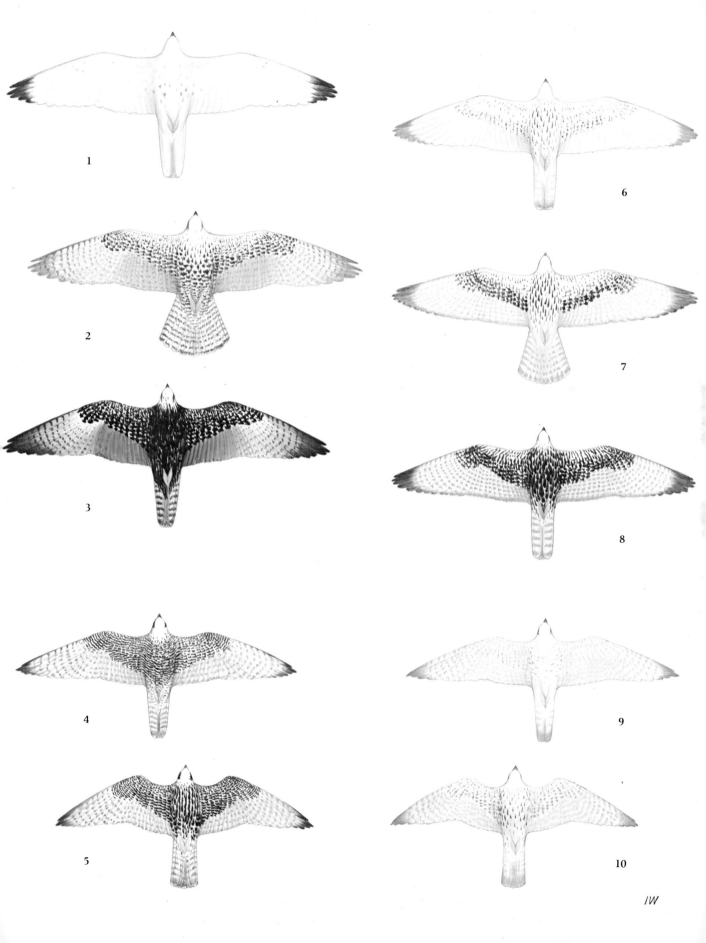

1

6

2

7

3

8

4

9

5

10

IW

Bibliography

Bijleveld, M. (1974). *Birds of Prey in Europe*. London.

Brown, L. and Amadon, D. (1968). *Eagles, Hawks and Falcons of the World*. Country Life Books, London.

Cramp, S. and Simmons, K.E.L. (eds.) (1980). *Handbook of the Birds of Europe, the Middle East, and North Africa: The Birds of the Western Palearctic*, Vol. II. Oxford University Press.

Greenway, J.C. (1958). *Extinct and Vanishing Birds of the World*. Special Publication 13. American Committee for International Wild Life Protection, New York.

Meinertzhagen, R. (1959). *Pirates and Predators*. Oliver and Boyd, Edinburgh.

Moore, N.W. (1957). *British Birds* Vol. 50, pp. 173–97.

Moreau, R.E. (1972). *The Palaearctic–African Bird Migration Systems*. Academic Press, London.

Porter, R.F., Willis, I., Christensen, S., and Nielsen, B.P. (1981). *Flight Identification of European Raptors* (3rd edn). Poyser, London.

Welty, J.C. (1962). *The Life of Birds*. Saunders, Philadelphia.

Index

Page numbers for descriptions accompanied by plates are bold type, thus: **24**.

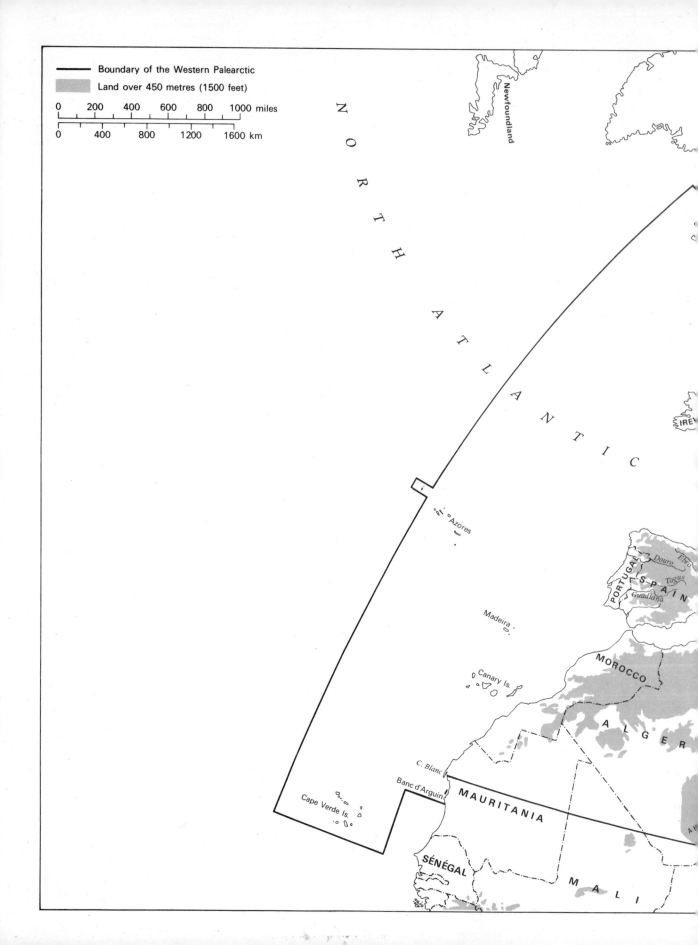

0   200   400   600   800   1000 miles

0   400   800   1200   1600 km

N O R T H

Newfoundland

A T L A N T I C

IRE

Azores

PORTUGAL   SPAIN
Douro   Ebro
Tagus
Guadiana

Madeira .

MOROCCO

Canary Is.

A L G E R

C. Blanc

Banc d'Arguin

MAURITANIA

Cape Verde Is.

SÉNÉGAL

M A L I